sweet spirit

COMBINED VOLUME

SWEET SPIRIT SERIES

DONNA GODDARD

Copyright © 2024 by Donna Goddard

All rights reserved. No part of this book may be reproduced in any form or by any electronic or mechanical means, including information storage and retrieval systems, without written permission from the author, except for the use of brief quotations in a book review.

contents

Sweet Spirit: Combined Volume   vii
Opening Prayer   ix

TOUCHED BY LOVE

Introduction   3

PART ONE
BODY
HOLDER OF OUR LIFE FORCE

1. Spotlights   7
   Body
2. Perfect   34
3. Ownership   39
4. Beloved Basket   41
5. Compulsion   43
6. Good Night, Sleep Tight   45
7. Sly Deceiver: Isobel and Benedict   47
   Story

PART TWO
RELATIONSHIPS
WHAT WE VALUE

8. Spotlights   55
   Relationships
9. Tools for Growth   94
10. The Rise After the Fall   97
11. Price of Love   101
    Devotion
12. Can You Love Too Much?   105
13. The Bigger Person   107
    Forgiveness

14. Right On Cue	108
15. Thanks Love	110
16. Karma and the Beggar	113
17. Conscious Use	115
18. Enemies *Question and Answer*	117
19. Another Chance: Bethany and Daniel *Story*	120
20. Wild Beast Spirit: Dahlia and the Shepherd *Story*	126

PART THREE
SPIRITUAL PATH
ENTIRELY SELFISH

21. Spotlights *Spiritual Path*	131
22. Top Tips	156
23. Spiritual Processes	158
24. Reality Shifting	161
25. Miraculous Stats *Zero to Hero*	163
26. No Martyrs	166
27. Light Bearers *Hands-on-Healing*	169
28. Energy Centres *Energy Healing*	172
29. Angels from the Dust	175

LOVE MATTERS

Introduction	179

PART ONE
PHYSICAL MATTERS
BODY AND ITS ENVIRONMENT

1. Spotlights *Body*	183
2. Elemental	198

3. Body and Spiritual Practices	216
4. Home	220
5. Face Value	222
6. Don't Give Your Sleep Away	225
7. Wheeling and Dealing	227
8. Frictionless Fields	229
9. Living and Dying	232
10. Sweet Destroyer: Saleha and Mirko *Story*	235

PART TWO
PEOPLE MATTERS
WHOLE HOLY RELATIONSHIPS

11. Spotlights *Relationships*	241
12. Forgiveness	261
13. Being Liked	264
14. Shining Through	266
15. Our Dearest Friends	269
16. Way, Wayward, and Wayless	271
17. It Was Only Natural: Millie and Emerson *Story*	273
18. How Did He Ever Find You: Amy and Mervin *Story*	277

PART THREE
MYSTIC MATTERS
HEALING AND SPIRITUAL HAPPINESS

19. Spotlights *Spiritual Path*	283
20. Healing *Helpful or Haywire*	316
21. Primary Practices	331
22. Choose Consciousness	334
23. Translating	338
24. Fear is Your Friend	340
25. Awake and Aware	342
26. Humans are Aliens Too	344

27. Spiritual Teachers	346
28. Garden Your Consciousness	350
Closing Prayer	353
Sweet Spirit Series	355
About the Author	357
Also by Donna Goddard	359

sweet spirit: combined volume

This is the combined volume of the

SWEET SPIRIT SERIES

Touched by Love (Book 1)
Love Matters (Book 2)

opening prayer

I unreservedly dedicate
the time spent
reading and reflecting
on this book
to my spiritual growth
for my own benefit
and the benefit of all those
who come near me
or even think of me.

touched by love

BOOK 1 OF SWEET SPIRIT SERIES

introduction

Touched by Love is about our body, relationships, and the spiritual path. It is vital to maintain, understand, and balance each of them. We must strengthen, expand, and extend all the energetic systems of our being. It takes work and commitment, but that is the purpose of life.

1. **Body**: The body is the holder of our life force. Protect, value, and use it, but don't think it is an end in itself. We must work with every level of our being to make it more harmonious, efficient, and effective. Make a sacred space out of your body, mind, and spirit. Refine them every day with whatever practices work best for you. Don't ignore one aspect of your being out of laziness, ignorance, resentment or resistance.
2. **Relationships**: The price of a successful relationship is devotion. Devotion is, essentially, commitment to something we value. What are we devoted to? Surely not what another person wants. Most people would agree that being

devoted to that would be problematic even with the best of people. So, what exactly are we devoted to? We are devoted to the well-being of another person. And we are devoted to the well-being of the relationship. We honour the other person's value and the relationship's worth.

3. **Spiritual Path**: No one has to be a martyr on the spiritual path. On the contrary, everyone should be entirely selfish. Not selfish in the usual sense of the word, but selfish in the way of knowing that the spiritual path means we value everything that adds to our well-being.

> When we love, we live with connectedness.
> When we forgive, we feel stress-free.
> When we create, we live with inspiration.
> When we follow inner direction, we feel alive.
> Is that even a choice?

PART ONE

body

HOLDER OF OUR LIFE FORCE

CHAPTER 1

spotlights

BODY

BODY AND PHYSICAL STRUCTURES

LIFE FORCE

The body is the holder of our life force. Protect, value, and use it, but don't think it is an end in itself.

CONSCIOUSNESS

To be healthy and happy, we only have to do one thing. Be conscious. If we are conscious, we will work everything out.

1. We will work out that our body needs exercise, good food, connection with nature, and attention to any problems we may acquire along the way.
2. We will know that our emotional being needs to give and receive love and must be committed to the practice of compassion. Grudges are a killer in every way.
3. We will sense what to do next on a path most suited to our spiritual needs.

WORK ON IT

You can't make progress without some amount of struggle. If you want a stronger body, you have to make it work, and that involves some discomfort. If you want better relationships, you have to connect at a deeper level, and that can be uncomfortable. If you want a more evolved consciousness, you have to work on the stuff that comes up, and that is generally confronting. Do it anyway. You and your evolution and happiness are worth it.

MORE ONE THAN THE OTHER

When you are born, you do not leave your spirit behind and become a body. You are always a spirit, and so is everyone else. That is why you can never be separated from anyone. Once on Earth, if you can remember that you are mostly spirit, you will have a great power to create a wonderful world for yourself and everyone else.

OWNERSHIP

Your soul belongs to the Divine, but your body belongs to the earth.

FEELING NOTHING

A well body does not feel well. It feels nothing. It efficiently, effectively, and without complaint does whatever we ask it to do, and that's all. It's neither well nor sick. It is a manifestation of our thoughts that we can use for the purposes we decide. This approach is not only useful in healing, but it is also useful to people who want to perform at a top physical level because they have a different way of viewing their body.

LISTEN AND LEARN

Try to become conscious of what you eat and why you are eating it at that particular moment. Every body's needs are different and will change with the seasons and from day to day. Listen to your body in the same way that animals do. They instinctively know what to eat and what to reject in their natural habitat. This will benefit your health enormously.

FOOD

Like everything else in life, we should eat consciously. We should learn to listen to our body about what to eat, how much (not too much or too little), and about foods that will not strain or poison our system. If the communication channel is clear between body and mind, we will know what we need for our body-type, age, activity level, and health issues. We can still treat ourselves with things we love, but we should do so in honest moderation and with awareness. Eating what is suitable for our individual system keeps our body healthy and active and our mind awake and alert.

PRANA

Try to use the stovetop more often and the microwave less. Although microwaving is fast and convenient, it changes the prana in food. The guide is home-cooked, slow and low heat.

DAILY BREAD

If bread is one of your staple carbohydrate foods, which it is for most people in the West, then think carefully about what you are buying. Many breads in the supermarket are "old" in the sense of not being made that day and/or having preservatives in them. You want one of your main staple foods to be made that day and have no preservatives. Apart from that, try different breads to see which has the most beneficial effect on your body's functioning. When I move houses/towns, I try maybe twenty different breads from all different shops until I find the one that is closest to what I want. Your bread becomes your body.

EXERCISE

We need to exercise daily and use our bodies to build health, strength, longevity, and aliveness. The physical body is the foundation of our existence here. If it is not doing well, we will struggle to find the necessary resources to put into the other components of life. All the levels of our being—physical, mental, emotional, and spiritual—should be fed, protected, nurtured, and cherished for the valuable way they serve us and facilitate our happiness.

BODY-CLAY

In yoga, qigong, or any physically demanding discipline, we turn our body back into clay so that it can be remade how we want it. At the same time, we can also remake our mental and ethereal bodies.

LESS BODY

Try to see yourself more as energy and less as body. Unlike body, energy has the ability to transform instantly and in whichever direction it seeks to move. Unlike body, the possibilities of energy are limitless, astounding, exciting, and altogether marvellous.

MANY MAKINGS

The first making of ourselves from birth to young adulthood is generally unconscious. It follows nature's instinctive inbuilt mechanism. The second making (or remaking) of ourselves can be entirely conscious.

FULL AND FREE

We must balance the masculine and feminine within ourselves. Masculine power and feminine love are much more than gender and sexual behaviour. Balancing the masculine and feminine elements gives us the ability to fully and freely function as whole individuals.

HASTY HEALING

We should not be too quick to heal physical and mental discomfort in ourselves and others. The pain is trying to tell us something important. If we find a way to delete the problem without understanding its message, it will often return in a worse form. It's better to patiently work with the problem until it dissolves in its own way. Thus, we will benefit from the entire process.

PAIN AS PATH INDICATOR

Be kind to yourself.
Pain is not a judgement.
It's a path indicator.

MATTERS MOST

Physical life is not as physical as it seems. Most of it is the space between the solid. The majority of what matters most in life requires neither space nor time. It is the stuff in between the physical:

- the breadth of ideas
- the depth of emotional connection
- the height of spiritual inspiration

BALANCED BRAIN

It's important to oscillate between left-brain and right-brain activities. Don't do one type of activity for too long without shifting focus. For example, as a writer, I spend a lot of time on my computer. However, I break up the day with other activities—walking, dancing, yoga, qigong, and meditation practices. Work out how much of your day is directed towards the physical, mental, and energetic. Every individual is made up differently and will require a different balance, but all areas are vital. If you neglect one, then in some way, you will become unbalanced and suffer.

SPACE

Spaces have energy. They are not neutral and will affect the state of your mind and body. Maintaining an active, positive, harmonious mental climate or energy field in your home is important. Many people do this instinctively. It's more difficult to keep the energy of larger homes alive. Don't assume that bigger is better. From an energetic perspective, it's easier to keep the energy of a smaller living space imbued with the right dynamic.

No matter what size space you live in, keep it clean and uncluttered. Don't hold onto things if their day is done. Think in terms of energy, not acquisition. Being conscious of the energetic atmosphere of your home will be highly beneficial to you and your family's well-being.

FOCUSED INTELLIGENCE

Animals are not less intelligent than humans. They are a very focused intelligence. A snake is brilliant at being a snake. No one can be a snake better than a snake.

MONEY

Our world is evolving towards an economic state where money (including digital) is not the primary medium of exchange. In a more harmonious, happier, and higher level civilisation, individuals do whatever they are capable of and enjoy in exchange for what they need. Some exchanges can be via an economic system, but much of what people need will come through other types of exchange. The synchronistic alignment of life will flourish. Giving and getting are, in essence, a matter of energy transfer.

WEALTH

Many years ago, I went to a self-development talk, and the speaker asked the large audience, "Raise your hand if you are wealthy." As expected, a small proportion of people put up their hands. There was something irresistible about the question. Wealthy? How could I leave my hand down as if I was one of the unfortunate ones missing out on something valuable? My hand shot up. Later, my friend said, "I didn't know you had money!" I said, "I don't."

On more than one occasion, one of my sons said, "When I look back on how much money we lived on, it wasn't much, but I never felt like that. I always felt that we had enough to do whatever we needed to do."

That is the definition of abundance—*To have enough to do*

what you genuinely need to do in life, which could be anything, as every person is different.

MOUTH MOVEMENT

Say less, but mean more with what you say. It's a practice, a discipline. It will make you more aware. Your presence will become more beneficial.

ATTRACTIVENESS

The most attractive thing in the universe is to care.

INTIMACY

True intimacy is not a physical act but a state of nonresistance, nonjudgment, and acceptance between individual people.

TOUCHING

Travel inwards.
Make yourself spectacular
on the inside.
Touch everyone with that.

Bodies touching is skin-deep,
although it has its place.
Minds touching is enlargening.
Souls touching is infinite expansion.

NATURE

DAY, WEEK, MONTH, YEAR

Once a day, go outside to a park or nature reserve and set yourself up for the day. Once a week, go outside your city. Spend a few hours in rawer nature, which will set you up for the week. Once a month, go further afield and spend the night. Don't do anything in particular except listen and let the natural order set you up for the month. Once a year, go somewhere entirely different and set up your life course. It will remind you that life is diverse, expansive, and complex. It will make you feel small (in the best way) so that life can be seen as an exciting, endless possibility.

NETWORK

The plants on our planet are the creators of the environment in which we live. They have many more abilities of sense than we realise. They are not individual entities existing on their own. They have a vast intercommunication system underneath the surface of the soil through their root system. Also, they reach into the air and transfer energy and life force from one to the other. They are a living, working community. If we understand our vital relationship with plants, we will respect, honour, and protect them.

MORE FOREST

When you are worried, go to the forest. We and our worries get smaller as everything else gets more.

TREE TALK

When the world bothers you, talk to an old tree. The older, the better. It always puts things in perspective.

PLAY

Play with life. Kick the pile of autumn leaves. Jump the river rocks. Play the game. Laugh loudly. Kiss freely. Let the child in you rise and thrive.

TOUCH THE EARTH

> *Touch the earth.*
> *Feel the sun.*
> *Listen to the passing wind.*
> *Let the healing power*
> *of nature restore you.*

MAKING FRACTIONS WHOLE

The very process of being alive means being constantly inundated with fractious elements that work against our body's integrity. We need a healthy, quiet body to do whatever we came to do. Touching the earth is one of the quickest, most effective ways of helping our body restore itself.

LITTLE SEEDS

Autumn and spring are times for growth. The gentler weather provides ideal conditions. Like seeds, we need light, warmth, and proper nourishment for our well-being. We need it as a body, on an emotional level, and as a soul. Tend to all the layers of your being so you can grow and thrive.

BEING IN SYNC

If we are in sync with nature, we will be in sync with ourselves. We belong to Heaven, but we are made from earth.

AT HOME

When we are at home in ourselves, we are at home in the whole universe.

CATCHING RAYS

An excellent spiritual practice (and one that comes naturally to many people who are in tune with life) is to catch the first rays of the sun. Your body, being nature, instinctively wants to be awake when the day begins. It doesn't like to miss the beginning of the day's story.

DAY AND NIGHT TRANSITIONS

Our body will be more grounded and problem-free if we train ourselves to be aware of the day/night transitions at dawn and dusk. The more stable we are as a body, the more freedom we will have to explore life's subtler, finer dimensions. The higher dimensions make us receptive, empathic, creative, and joyful.

LOOKING

> Look up. Look down.
> Look in. Look out.
> The more aware we are,
> the more alive we become.

CLEANERS

Wind and water are the cleaning agents of nature. We need them as humans as much as nature needs them.

CHILDREN OF SUN AND MOON

Fall in love with the moon.
We need its balance.
Find its hiding place in the day
and be mesmerised by
its graceful potency at night.

Stay close to the sun.
We are only here because of it.
Walk every morning and
become a sun-soaked, sun-raised,
sunbeam child of light.

NATURE'S NATURE

The nature of nature is to heal and energise. Whenever we give it a little time and attention, it dissolves our problems, realigns our body, clears our mind, and awakens our spirit. And it's free. In return, we need to protect it, but we are simply protecting our own future.

NATURE'S EASE

We get fixated on various aspects of life, insisting that they must work in specific ways. Inevitably, they don't work in the particular ways we have outlined. The great benefit of connecting with nature is that it doesn't insist on anything. Yet, it is highly functional and successful.

FORCE OF NATURE

Become a force of nature. The entire range of nature's existence runs through your DNA. Your parentage is incontestable.

STILL POINT

Many people find that the easiest and quickest way to reach their *still point* is in nature. There is a tremendous amount of stillness in the busyness of nature. If we can find the still point in nature, we can find it in our bodies. Our body is nature. The still point in nature is also the still point in us.

UNMUDDLED PLACE

To create what we want in our lives, we must first clear our mind so that it is an unmuddled place to manifest. Nature is very conducive to this purpose. Once your mind is clear, let your consciousness form its own goals from your deepest being. Start with goals that are personal to you. Then, create bigger ones. Ensure that all your goals, from individual to extensive, do not harm anyone and benefit all.

You must keep returning to your goals to ensure they are alive, energetic, focused, and on track. Each time you return with mental clarity and focused energy, they will grow and have more power to manifest, often beyond what you originally envisaged.

AGEING AND DEATH

VEHICLE

If we want a long and productive life, we must take special care of the vehicle God gave us to move around in while we are here. Abuse, neglect, and lack of maintenance will come back to repay us with pain, lethargy, dysfunction, and a shorter-than-possible lifespan. Paying attention to our consciousness evolution is difficult if we have physical discomfort. When the body is comfortable and silent, we can more easily focus on higher pursuits.

TIME AND THE BODY

The more we are attached to our physical body, the more problematic time will be for us. If we hold our body loosely (like a well-selected, well-cared-for piece of clothing that is comfortable and suits us), we will find that time goes by quickly and peacefully.

RENEWABLE ENERGY

Your mind and spirit are very capable of healing your body. Your body is a constantly renewing entity. Ride through life with this knowledge and practice, and a remarkable number of problems will transform into blessings.

LOSING THE SPARK

Most people age much earlier than necessary. By thirty, many are old inside. By forty, most have lost the spark of life. By fifty, they are already senior. All of this is entirely preventable and, to a large extent, reversible.

TRANSFORMATION

Learn to see yourself as energy rather than body. Energy constantly renews and transforms. How, where, and why it transforms is a complex matter, but there is no question of its ending.

USE OR LOSE

Ageing happens at all levels of our being, but the body is the most obvious. Use it or lose it. One of the reasons I dance, apart from my love of it, is that my teachers (who are generally younger than me) push me to keep using my body in ways that I might not otherwise. In large dance classes, I often intentionally stand next to the twenty-year-old, exuberant dancers, as their energy (of which they have masses to spare) helps me.

INTERGENERATIONAL

Young children and senior citizens often go together beautifully due to the energy exchange. The elderly gain fuel from young life, and the attentive, stable energy of seniors calms little children.

MARCH OF TIME

You will be fighting a losing battle if you only exercise your body and not your mind and spirit. When you use them all, they will gladly and efficiently work together. Although we cannot completely stop the march of time on our use-by-stamped bodies, we can have the blessings of a well-functioning and alive body, an active and bright mind, and a loving and expressive soul.

ADDING OR SUBTRACTING YEARS

Practice burning up the day's resentments when lying in bed at night. If you look carefully, you will find numerous small and large grievances from the day—not to mention the enormous backlog. If you are not ready to reduce the past baggage, at least don't add another day to it. Tell yourself that whatever happened today, you will dissolve. You will sleep better and automatically sort out physical and mental health issues at night without knowing. It will add years and health to your life in the same way that grievances detract years and health from your life.

MORTALITY

> *The realisation of our mortality puts us on the spiritual path. Remembering it keeps us there.*

GAME OF LIFE

If you didn't know your age, what would you guess it was by how your body feels? This is a fun and useful question to help you estimate the state of your current physical health. Interestingly, people tend to perceive us as being around the age at which we perceive ourselves.

NUMBERED

Your days are numbered. Don't spend them in avoidance and fear, or you will get to your last one and regret that so many were unopened and untried, unused and undervalued.

LIFE FRAGILITY

Once we understand the fragility of life, we live more consciously. We don't have enough time for fighting, hating, scheming, holding back, procrastinating, and numbing ourselves with various tranquillisers. We need to use it to better ourselves and the world we inhabit.

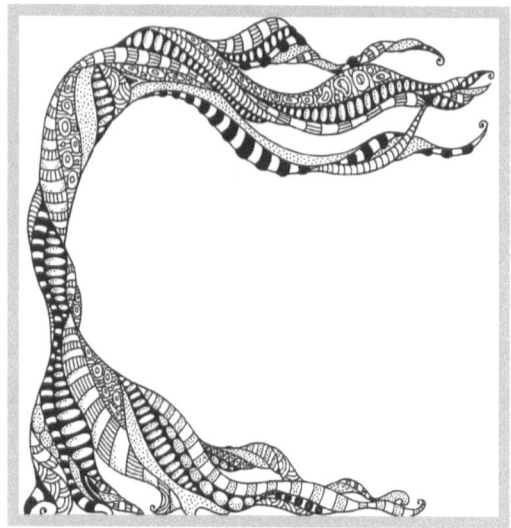

LIFE-LOAN

Death is not a possibility for the soul. However, the earth vessel the soul uses is definitely on loan. It must be entirely given back at a specified time. While we have the loan, we should make the most of it. We should do what we are sincerely interested in, love fully, protect ourselves from those who wish us harm, and find joy in the spectacular gift of this lifetime.

WASTING YEARS

We generally don't like to be reminded that, sooner or later, we are going to die. However, having this thought in the back of our minds helps us to live well. My father's sudden death when I was seventeen significantly impacted my decision to live life how I sincerely wanted to. Otherwise, laziness, apathy, fear, indecision, and delusion can waste not only years but a whole lifetime.

CERTAIN DEATH

Only those who have crossed paths with death ponder the meaning of life. From the moment we are born, our passing is assured. Everything else in life is subject to change. But this one thing is sure. We shall, one day, leave. We live fully and love fearlessly only when we understand our mortal nature. We throw ourselves into life because we are not here for long.

GOOD WORKING ORDER

Genetic issues aside, the body and all its parts are designed to last our lifetime. Keep it in good working order, and it will serve you well until the end. When that end comes, design your parting so that you move out of your body gently and peacefully. You came into your first home (your mother) without drama. You can leave the same way.

BRIEF TIME

If we remind ourselves that we are here briefly, our choices become more meaningful, appropriate to our individuality, and satisfying. We don't have to be told to stay in contact with the Divine when we know that we must make this life count.

ANOTHER DAY

If you are reading this, it means that you are alive. You have been given another day of life. Be grateful. If we do not take being here for granted, we will be more inclined to make the most of our time. We don't have to *do* more. We have to listen more—in the right way. Then our doing will not be a burden but a pleasure.

LIVE PASSIONATELY

If we want to truly experience life, we must play with it. Without passion, there will be no fire for life. The spark will grow dim and dull and eventually go out. Everything worthwhile carries risk. Live your life passionately.

TOUCHED BY LOVE

CHAPTER 2

perfect

My doctor didn't beckon me into her consulting room with her usual cheery greeting. Noted but unconcerned, I entered.

She paused for dramatic effect and said, "I suppose you could tell by my message that it isn't good news."

She looked at me to make sure that I was suitably attentive. The receptionist had phoned a few days earlier, asking me to make an immediate appointment to discuss test results. I explained that I was interstate visiting family. I was told that a few days' wait would be fine. Then I filed the issue in the back of my mind and felt all would be well.

A worried frown seemed the only appropriate response now. The doctor explained that I needed to have a skin area removed and that the specialist clinic would call me within a day. She added that I should tell my loved ones.

Confused and unsure how much of life and death was at stake, I said, "No, I'll tell them when everything is fine."

"You must tell them now," insisted the doctor.

I nodded but had no intention of doing so. I love my doctor. She's great, but she *is* a doctor.

A couple of days later, after reading the information from the Skin Clinic, I realised that the prognosis was much more optimistic than my doctor had inferred, and the Clinic was confident that it could be handled successfully with day surgery. With renewed assurance that I would be around for the foreseeable future, I mentioned to my adult children that I had a minor medical issue that needed to be sorted out in the coming days. Done.

The day arrived. I was very nervous. Other than births, I've had very little medical intervention in my life, preferring to heal things in holistic ways, if possible. Anyway, I don't think anyone feels comfortable with the thought of being cut open for medical reasons, even when we are grateful for the necessary intervention. Instinct tells us to protect our body. It is the precious and irreplaceable holder of the life force which allows us the privilege of human existence.

The Clinic staff were professional and pleasant. All was going calmly. Until the intake nurse, that is. She seemed to find many mistakes on my long intake form, which she resented having to fix. Then she took my blood pressure.

She turned to me with an accusatory glare and said, "Your blood pressure is *very* high." Pointing to my body, she added, "You are a little person. It should be much lower. You need to see your doctor as soon as possible to address this."

She waited for a response, so I mumbled, "Is it high? It's not normally. I don't think it is anyway."

Suddenly, I felt I had no idea what my blood pressure normally was. Maybe, I didn't know anything about my body. Maybe, I was reckless. Maybe, I had a serious heart issue as well as a skin issue. Maybe, my heart would kill me before anything else had a chance to. Panic was reigning supreme. I could feel my heart pumping wildly in my chest. I'm sure it would have doubled if she had retaken my blood pressure.

Somehow, a small voice entered my racing brain, and I said to her, "I am nervous. Could that make it go up?"

She looked at me over her glasses and said, "You don't look nervous."

Feeling a spark of anger at her scare-monger tactics toward vulnerable patients, I thought, *No, I don't **look** nervous. I'm trained not to look nervous. I'm trained to do terrifying Dancesport competitions and look as cool as a cucumber. And long before that, I was professionally trained to listen to people's problems and remain calm, helpful, and encouraging. No, I don't look nervous because I'm a mother and have had years of helping offspring with all manner of life's problems (even ones that make you want to cry to their face but, of course, you don't).*

Later, when I was settled into the operating room with several bright and positive medical professionals, I mentioned the high blood pressure as I still wasn't sure if it was a problem.

The wonderful surgeon said with a hint of smile, "You are excited."

"I'm nervous," I explained.

She smiled more broadly and said, "Nonsense, you are just excited!"

We both laughed, and thus the scene was set for a quick, successful, and painless procedure.

Before she did the incision, I must have had a panicked look on my face. One of the nurses asked kindly, "Are you okay?"

I took hold of her steady hand. She instantly responded by holding mine reassuringly and, for good measure, put her other hand on my arm.

I thought, *This is why it is much better to have caring, well-trained professionals in situations like this rather than loved ones. We don't want to worry family members, so we don't say if we need help. Anyway, the fear in their eyes exacerbates the problem.*

There is a tradition in parts of India that dying people go to a holy place to leave this life, rather than doing so in the presence of their family. Family ties can drag out the leaving process, making the transition more complicated. Maybe, that's why many animals (like cats) prefer to go into isolation and hide (if they can) when they are unwell.

In the operating theatre, the nurses, other than the hand-holding one, took over the necessary jobs, and my hand-holder became the resident entertainment. She was a natural-born storyteller.

Raised on a farm with her nine siblings, they had a great assortment of animals. Her father brought home a tiny, deserted baby animal at one stage. It was so young that they couldn't tell what it was. After bottle-feeding it, they eventually discovered it was a fox. His favourite place to sleep was with the rottweiler. When the fox grew up, he made a den under the farmhouse. Every evening, he would trot off to hunt and, every morning, return to get a piece of "mother's best bacon" from Dad. One day, he didn't return. Dad said that he had probably found a girlfriend. Later, my nurse friend realised that the local farmers were always shooting foxes and made the connection to her own loved foxy-family member.

This young woman had the story-telling capacity of James Herriot of *All Creatures Great and Small,* who wrote about his humorous, heartening animal adventures in rural England around the 1930s.

Interrupting the stories, which had only just begun, the surgeon said that all was finished and that she shouldn't need to see me again. Before they released me, one of the nurses retook my blood pressure.

She pointed to the number on the machine and said, "See, it's perfect."

CHAPTER 3

ownership

A few years ago, I was walking with my oldest son along a Sydney harbourside path in a wealthy suburb.

After talking about the beautiful properties, I said, "I think I have lost the sense of ownership."

"What do you mean?" he asked.

"Of course, we have to survive, but, in essence, I've lost the desire to own things," I continued. "Owning as a concept has become somewhat meaningless to me."

"Can you give an example?" he asked.

"Disregarding any relevant practical matters, the idea of owning a house rather than renting one has lost its meaning to me. I can no more own it than not own it."

I looked around and pointed across the road at a magnificent multi-million-dollar house.

"See that house," I said. "I feel I could walk into it and own it as much as the owners, or rather, not own it as much as the owners."

"I'm not sure they would feel the same way," he laughed.

CHAPTER 4

beloved basket

At one stage, I had an IKEA laundry basket with a divider marked for light and dark clothes. It was a cheap basket, but when I found it, it was a great answer to a laundry problem I had had for years. I had a busy home life with a partner, teenage children, and a young child. The house had a lot of laundry, and it all went into one basket. The bathroom had no room for two baskets (one for light clothes and one for dark). Then, one day, I found the marvellous invention of a compact, divided, upright clothes basket that would fit in the bathroom. It meant that everyone could sort their own clothes into the relevant sections.

Eventually, my house got much quieter, but for some reason, I couldn't part with the no longer needed laundry basket. One day, it dawned on me that the basket had acquired good karmic energy from being such a loved and useful item. Realising this, I was finally able to part with my beloved basket. Rest in peace, old friend.

CHAPTER 5

compulsion

The vast majority of what people do on a physical, mental, and emotional plane comes from embedded, unconscious reactiveness or compulsion. Compulsiveness means to do something unconsciously, often without being aware that one is doing it, let alone why one is doing it. Eating, sexual activity, pornography, drinking alcohol, drug taking, medication popping, T.V. watching, social media scrolling, working excessively, talking too much (and most talking is too much), shopping, and worrying fall into the compulsive basket for many people.

Fighting compulsiveness won't work. The compulsion will only get stronger or be directed into another compulsion. While we shouldn't fight compulsions, we shouldn't blindly follow them either. What will work is to understand the healing process.

Have you noticed that when you are happy, you are not compulsive? However, when sad, angry or fearful thoughts are trying to surface (and you don't want them to), your behaviour will automatically tend to become compulsive. Compulsions try to cover up unpleasant, uncomfortable, painful thoughts.

We should try to understand what the compulsion is specifically stemming from. If we do this sincerely, particular painful thoughts will rise to the surface of our minds. Don't be afraid of them or scared of the emotion attached to them. Let them come up. Look at them. Feel the emotion. Give it a protected space to rant and rave, tremble and shiver, mope and drag.

After you've looked at the thoughts, memories, and emotions enough, reassure yourself with whatever spiritual teachings are dear to you. You are loved, and there is a force looking after even your smallest concerns. The compulsion will gradually lessen (sometimes, instantaneously disappear), and you will feel lighter and happier.

CHAPTER 6

good night, sleep tight

You can learn to use your sleep for restoration, healing, and inspiration:

1. Last thing at night, hand yourself over to the Divine or any higher being you are connected to. As your skill increases, you can ask for sleep-time answers to problems or inspired ideas. They may come to you in dreams, or you may become aware of specific thoughts (particularly shortly before waking).
2. If you want to manifest something, such as a business idea, a relationship goal, or any other goal, think of it lightly before sleep. Then, humbly, without interference, hand it to Source. It helps to say, "I'm not insisting that this happens, but this is what I draw towards myself. I would like it for my benefit and the benefit of other people." Have confidence that your prayer is answered. See it as answered. Go to sleep as if you have the thing you desire for your well-being and fulfilment.

3. If you have a nightmare or feel unwell in the night, don't roll over lazily and hope for the best as you surrender yourself back to sleep. You will be going back into a battle. And you won't be winning. Get up, make yourself warm, and devote a little time to looking at what has troubled you. Ask for Divine assistance in understanding and finding peace. Some of the best progress people make in their journey is in the middle of the night—alone, when everyone is asleep, and God has your undivided attention.

> *Tonight, before you drift into slow theta brainwaves, commit your sleep to positive purposes and ask the higher powers to guide, protect, and heal you.*

CHAPTER 7

Sly deceiver: isobel and benedict

STORY

Isobel watched Benedict walk unsteadily down his driveway towards the builders in the backyard. He hadn't dressed properly. He had no underwear on. His track pants were ripped so that anyone who looked (perhaps it was impossible not to look) could see his backside. Somehow, it was still a good-looking backside for all he had put his body through in recent years. There was no point telling him that he hadn't dressed properly. He was too sick. Along the way, things like dignity get lost.

The builders had been there for some weeks making a pool. Benedict wasn't short of money. It would have been better if he had been because the necessities of life would have pulled him back into some normality. The builders knew that Isobel was Benedict's ex-partner. Benedict repeated himself a lot. He reran stories incessantly in his head and out loud to anyone in his vicinity.

When Benedict stumbled back into the house, the head builder turned to Isobel and said, "I don't know why we are building this bloody pool. He will only fall into it in a drunken stupor and drown himself!"

Isobel said nothing. They all knew that the possibility of that happening was all too real.

A young apprentice lifted his head as Isobel headed for the house and said hopefully, "You've come to fix him up."

He meant to sound light-hearted, but the pity in his voice was unmistakable. Many people, even strangers, seemed to want to help Benedict. Isobel always found that very heart-warming. She didn't want to disillusion the young apprentice, so she smiled reassuringly and nodded as if that was what she had come to do.

She braced herself to enter the house. Any trace of smile left her face. It was worse than usual. Things were everywhere. The fridge door was left open. It was a pigsty. When she passed the bedroom, she was shocked to see blood on the wall, a broken mirror on the ground, and a hole in the plaster. She couldn't remember seeing any new injury on Benedict. Perhaps it was someone else's blood. That was even worse. It was pointless cleaning any of it up. She had done that many times. This time, it was just too dreadful.

After a while, Benedict slumped onto the lounge and said, head in hands, "I know I need help."

Isobel had heard it before, but he still wouldn't go to rehab. The terrible thing about rehab is not so much the physical withdrawal from alcohol or drugs. That is its own special kind of drama. The real terror is what is inside the person without any sedation: pain, longing, hopelessness, memories, anger, and fear. Isobel washed a mug, made Benedict a cup of tea, and left. What else could she do? He wasn't a minor. He wasn't mentally ill. He wasn't sick enough for a hospital. He wasn't dead, yet. It was his right, as an adult, to destroy himself.

Alcohol and drugs are the sly deceivers, thought Isobel, *coming in like a party and then way outstaying their welcome. The longer they stay, the less their hosts can see them.* The thought of putting a poisonous substance into one's body with the intention of losing one's normal state of awareness seemed very foreign to her.

Users often say that alcohol or drugs have no adverse effect on them. Every medication has a side effect. Alcohol and drugs are the most readily available, socially supported, and popular choice of medication. People embrace them like a trusted friend. For some people, like Benedict, they become a full-on addiction. Their deadly hold becomes a serious fight for survival. They will take everything. No mercy.

A few weeks later, Benedict changed his mind (what was left of it) and went to rehab. It was the first of many stays. The battle was far from over, but the time it took for him to start drinking after rehabilitation became longer. The time it took for him to go back to rehab after relapses became shorter. He was not in the death zone for quite so long. He was slowly getting better.

"I'm so sorry," said Benedict with tears one day, "I'm so sorry for all of it."

Isobel didn't bother to hide the relief in her voice, "The only thing that matters is that you are getting better now."

"There are whole periods I cannot even remember," said Benedict.

Isobel smiled as if it was of no consequence but thought, *It's probably just as well!*

I WAS THERE

I walked with you,
I never left.
You thought I did,
but I did not.

Every step of the way,
every glass you held,
every spirit you took,
every thing you killed.

Right there with you,
watching it all.
Every stupid, destructive
heart-wrenching thing.

Still alive.
God only knows how.
Still alive.
I saw it all.

No, I wasn't gone,
I felt it too.
Knew every fear,
knew the despair.

Every bruise,
every cut,
every cry,
every damn bit.

Right there,
right there.
Never gone,
always there.

There was another who
watched as well.
The boy you loved,
he saw it too.

Said little, as he
knew not how
to talk of things so
brutal and raw.

You engraved him
on your wrist,
on your pulse,
so your heart

could recall
why it beat,
why to live,
not to die,
why to try.

PART TWO

relationships

WHAT WE VALUE

CHAPTER 8

Spotlights
RELATIONSHIPS

LOVE

BREATHING CREATURES

Relationships are living, breathing creatures with a life force of their own. They cannot be stuffed in a cupboard or placed on a mantelpiece. They are not an assumed right. They need to be tended with care. They need daily attention. Not forgotten, but neither spoiled. No doubt, they are time-consuming. However, the attentive, respectful, caring, and humorous time together feeds them. Without that, the person may still be there, but the relationship won't be.

NO DISTANCE OR TIME

Once you link your energy system with another person, whatever you do will directly affect the other person, whether they know it or not, are nearby or far away. Energy knows no distance, time, or even conscious awareness.

FULL LOVE

Both qualities are needed in life—intense love and the ability to see ourselves as completely whole. We are only half-loving if we do not love deeply, wholeheartedly, and unreservedly. But if we do not have an innate independence and ability to thrive on our own, the ups and downs of life and people will completely throw us.

RESPONSIVENESS

When we love someone, we don't think about what we do or don't want to do in response to their needs. If there is a need, we respond. We are responsive because we care.

IGNITE

When we love another person, it is *we* who love. The other may ignite our love, but it is we who decide to love. We need to magnify our decision to love whether people love us or not.

POWER

Love has power—to heal, release, protect, and make life happy.

EVERYONE

As spiritual students, we learn to love everyone. However, we have different types of relationships in our lives, and we act accordingly.

THINK AND CARE

A lot of everyday anger would disappear, or at least dissipate, by keeping in mind two simple ideas:

1. Think about the other person (their perspective)
2. Care about the other person (their well-being)

STATE OF MIND

Our ability to love has nothing to do with other people. It has everything to do with our state of mind. That is what we work on—our consciousness.

TRUST

If you want to know who you can trust, think of who is

willing to tell you things about yourself that you don't want to hear. Think of who is willing to say such things to you but still loves you. Their love for you is more than their need for you to like them.

SOMEONE YOU AREN'T

If something is not working for you, it's not because you are not good enough. It may well be that you are trying to be someone you are not. In which case, how can your success find you? It will be looking for someone you currently aren't!

ACCEPTANCE

Love begins with accepting the person as they are. That does not mean we accept bad behaviour or a lazy attitude towards life. Our primary focus is on loving the person, come what may. Part of love is helping them become the best they can be. We want the best for them, but our love is not dependent on it. Life, without any assistance from us, has its own teaching methods.

PIVOTAL POINT

Accepting things as they are and people as they are currently expressing themselves is a pivotal point in one's development. The vast majority of people have a constant stream of judgements, opinions, blame, self-justification and self-aggrandisement. The willingness to practice not having opinions, judgements, and reasons for everything gives your body and mind the opportunity to become a healthy, transparent space for peace.

GROWING CIRCLE

If we want to be seen as loving, we can't just act lovingly. We have to honestly care. Most everyone can sense the difference between a genuinely caring person and one who is not. To care is to empathise. The capacity to empathise is a developmental stage. We have to feel secure enough within ourselves to turn our attention to the problems and joys of other people. We realise that what happens in the life of another has a meaningful impact on our own. The more developed our consciousness, the larger the circle of those we care about.

DESIRABLE

If we want people to love us, it's not about making ourselves into more attractive, likeable, desirable creatures. It's about making ourselves into more loving beings. It's not about *us* at all. It's about the genuine needs of other people. The problem of not being loved will be solved. Further, the very question of whether we are loved or not will disappear from our thought processes.

NO SACRIFICE

To be loving is not a sacrifice. It is to become more connected with the vital, compassionate, energetic, and intelligent source of our existence.

SAME THING

Love is our greatest need—giving and receiving it. Our task is to learn how to do both beautifully until giving and receiving become the same.

A PLACE FOR ALL

Instead of competing with people in your environment, think of everyone as part of a well-functioning, harmonious family where each member can thrive and have their place.

SWIMMING IN LOVE

If we see ourselves as living within the context of love, as swimming in an ocean of love, then we can be more relaxed about the flow of love in life, where it comes from, and where it goes. Sometimes, it will move towards us. Sometimes, it will move away from us. All the while, we are still swimming, and the water of love surrounds us. So we can relax. We become love, not asking for it, not manipulating it, not afraid that it will leave. We are grateful and glad whenever someone else wishes to join that flow of love.

FULL FLOWER

We all want sweetness, beauty, harmony, exhilaration, and happiness. Don't search for it endlessly and fruitlessly in other people and circumstances. Become it yourself, with total commitment and full force. Your life will flower with tremendous potential.

NEED

WITH OR WITHOUT

It is crucial to our relationships that we understand the difference between love and need. If we need someone and they leave, we will blame them for not loving us as much as we supposedly loved them. If we acknowledge that we needed them more than they needed us, we will not blame them. We will make ourselves so that we need less and love more. Then, no one is likely to leave. If they do, it will be with our blessing because we want them to find their way in life, with us or without.

MORE THAN ALRIGHT

When it comes to relationships, if you don't have a secure confidence in yourself, you will be in constant fear or become an emotional tyrant. We have to know that, come what may, we will be alright. More than alright. That sort of confidence doesn't come from the personal ego. Egoic confidence is a mask of terror. True confidence comes from an innate trust that life will guide us every step of the way to what is best for us. It's the sort of confidence that no one can ever take away from us. It is humble and, unlike egoic confidence, has no trace of arrogance.

STABILITY

Relationships form from the soil of compatibility. Compatibility is the mutual meeting of needs, at least to some extent. However, the overriding milieu of a relationship must be a commitment to the well-being of the other person. A relationship focused on needs will become self-oriented and heartless

—like a business contract. If it is centred on emotion alone, it will be susceptible to many fluctuations and could easily be derailed by the heart's erratic movements. If it is based on a commitment to the well-being of the other person, there is automatic stability and purpose.

HONESTY AND NEED

We make alliances and relationships because of our physical, emotional, social, financial, professional and spiritual needs. We don't make them because of other people's needs. If we are honest, we will be grateful for whatever needs are met. We will not blame people if they are unable or unwilling to fulfil other needs. The unstated but fundamental basis of the arrangement is clear, at least to us. Only when we understand our motives can we form a life that benefits us and others. Honesty is power in terms of personal development.

TREAD WITH CARE

That which holds us together is delicate. Tread with care. Take nothing for granted. Appreciate what others give you, but don't give what you shouldn't.

REJECTION

Do not view rejection as a personal failure. There are at least two sides involved, ours and the other. What we want and what others want may not be the same. People have a right to be different to us. It is pointless to force anything because freedom of choice is essential for life to flourish. This is the case for both personal and professional. If we face a lot of rejection in any area of life, we must look at what we offer and improve ourselves so that people will want what we have to give. One whose presence is a solution, not a problem, will be wanted and valued.

SHUT UP

Here is a simple but effective practice that will significantly improve the depth and quality of your relationships. When people talk to you, you don't have a conversation in your mind about how it relates to something in your own life. Don't "listen" to get the conversation back to you. People don't have to know about your life unless they ask. Usually, they won't. Or if they do, it is generally a token effort. Don't be like that. Genuinely listen to what other people say. You will never be short of friends!

GOOD COMPANY

If we are happy alone, then we must be in good company. Take that good company to other people. Whether or not they appreciate it is their decision, but make sure you are part of the path to happiness, not the path to suffering.

POINT OF VIEW

If we see ourselves primarily from the point of view of our relationships (good, bad, and ugly), we will never be able to reach our full potential. While we deeply love those God gives us along the way, the most crucial ongoing relationship we will ever have is with our own Divine being. We were born as a single entity. We will face death on our own. And we must return to the Divine under our own steam. Never give that right and responsibility away to another person, and never take it from another. You will find that the respect and gratitude from those you do this for runs deep.

GOOD ENOUGH

Many people feel they are not good enough for certain people they aspire to have relationships with. We must get to the point of realising it all comes from inside us, not outside. Otherwise, we will be forever reaching for the wrong thing. We will try to make ourselves safer by attaching to people we believe are more robust than us. We need to find that strong centre inside ourselves. Then, other people will not feel we want to use them for our own purposes.

FAMILY

IMPACT

Our family is a place where we can profoundly impact other people. Try to make that impact as positive, life-enhancing, and encouraging as possible.

SAFETY

Make a circle around you where there, at least, you do not have to put energy into protecting yourself as you have to in the world. Hopefully, our families are this for us, as well as our most trusted friends and, if fortunate, our work environments.

NO DEAL

When it comes to money and relationships, don't treat it like a business transaction where you are trying to get a good deal. Definitely, don't try to make money from people you love. Think in terms of FAIRNESS. Ask yourself, "Would I feel this is fair if I were the other person?" Relationships are a place to share your love and your life. In this way, you will be blessed with many things, often including money.

IN OUR LIKENESS

If we make something beautiful, resilient, alive, strong, generous, and positive out of our body, mind, and spirit, our lives will be impactful. Those who do this find that the typical intense drive to reproduce and create children in their likeness will significantly lessen. They may still have children, but the choice will be conscious. While we adore our children, the most important thing we must leave in this world when we die is the energetic impact of our full, well-lived lives.

MAKING A HOME

When raising children, it is not "making memories" that matters. It is the making of a home. That home is us—the state of our mind and heart. We are what make up the memory of a child. Who we are, who we become as a parent and a person, and how we respond to them and their needs are the most critical element in setting them up for their venture into life. When raising a child, it is time to make ourselves into something as memorable as possible.

OBJECTIVE

My adult daughter finds it amusing that when I speak about her and her sibling's growing up years, I often say something to the effect of:

- "*When* I had children," (implying that I no longer do)
- "*the* children" (not my children)

It is a way of saying that child-raising is temporary and that the offspring do not, and never did, belong to me. It is objectifying in a good way.

ENERGY UNITS

I envisage a world where family units will be more fluid. It's not that the concept of family will disintegrate, but the reasons for forming and continuing the family unit will become broader and more fluid. The formation of a family usually comes from physical needs and the drive to create children. We should respect our biological makeup. However, in a more evolved world, the desire to procreate will decrease because people will have many other outlets for creation and loving connection. In a more developed world, the body's physical drives will not be the motivating factor for forming energy units capable of doing much more than providing basic needs. People create energy units when they couple and form families. Their formation and potential become infinitely more extensive and endlessly fascinating when seen from a higher perspective.

FALLING IN LOVE

FALL

You have to fall in love. Falling in love makes you malleable. It makes you new. You get fresh eyes. Growth is inevitable. Those who fall in love with nothing change nothing. When you fall in love, something becomes more important than yourself.

LOVERS

Everyone wants love—not necessarily to be loving (that involves the work of transformation), but to be loved. People feel they would be happy if they were loved and, in particular, loved by specific people. Firstly, most people aren't such great lovers (in any sense). Secondly, that approach doesn't work. We have to start with our inevitable inner pain. Then, we must look for a way to live that truly works. From this grows the capacity for sincere lovingness.

HEART

One factor determining where and to whom we give our energy and love is the presence or absence of receptivity. Does the person value our presence in their life? Do they listen to and think about what we say? Do they give us their time? Do they provide us with part of their heart? We don't need it all, but if we are to impact another being, we need a genuine part of it.

RIDE IT OUT

You can fall in love with multiple people in life. Ride it out. You might be married to them, or that could be the furthest thing. The important thing is not the falling in love or the falling out of love. It's the love. Love people. Love them regardless of their role in your life. And love yourself. Then, no matter what happens—what you create, what they create, and what you both create together as two distinct people—it will somehow work without building up more damaging karma.

TRUST

You cannot demand that another person trust and open themselves to you. Trust is automatically earned by experience of availability and sincere concern. Essentially, it is unselfishness. It cannot be pretended but must be felt and repeatedly relayed to another person. We must do this for our children, partner, friends, and the world around us.

COLOURFUL LIFE

Funny, touching, ridiculous, wise, and real conversations give us the critical moments in our relationships. While it is true that our happiness is our own making, it is also true that so much of the colour, brilliance, and interest of life comes from our connection to other people.

POWER OF LOVE

Falling in love with someone only has so much power. It's a lot, but eventually, the person has to want to grow. Falling in love is a powerful inroad into change, but it won't be enough on its own. People must be willing to love, change, and understand things better. Without that, no relationship survives and thrives in a functional, happy way.

CONFLICT AND PROBLEMS

BE SORRY, SAY SORRY

Most people make a lot of mistakes. We must learn how to not only be sorry but say sorry. When someone has the capacity to be sincerely sorry, almost anything is forgivable. Unfortunately, many people have such a fragile sense of themselves that they spend enormous effort developing defences. They will lose many relationships and end up suffering a lot. So tell yourself with simple humility, "I make mistakes. I'm a work-in-progress." And when appropriate, let people know you are sorry when you hurt them.

FEAR FACTOR

It is fear that makes people act in damaging and cruel ways. It is a misplaced sense of physical or emotional danger and inability to cope. Without realising this, the person will never break free from the cycle of their negative and demoralising behaviour.

COMMUNICATION

So much of what people say is not what they really think. Lack of authentic communication mostly comes from fear. We must learn to communicate honestly and with love. We must also learn to listen to the constant stream of silent words that move between and around us.

IT IS WHAT IT IS

Whenever we are upset about anyone or any situation, it helps to start from the premise that *it is what it is*. People are what they are at any given level of their understanding and will act accordingly. Once accepted, we can take responsibility for doing our best with our unique qualities and capabilities. We are responsible for our effort, not the outcome. Be assured that the outcome of any genuinely good effort, one way or another, is simply a matter of time. Life is always trying to align with its highest expression.

WHO

No person or partnership is worth betraying ourselves. If we choose a person or partnership over our true Self, little by little, we will die inside anyway. If we choose our truth, without fear or anger and with love for all, we will save ourselves and others along the way. *Who* we save is not our choice. It is theirs.

ARGUE WELL

A couple that can argue well can also live together well. This does not mean that arguing is valued in and of itself. However, conflict is inevitable when two different people try to share their lives at many different levels. It is imperative that neither is scared to speak up. It is vital that each can honestly say how they feel and what they think. Each must know that they are respected, even if disagreed with. Only in this way can a genuine, open, and deep bond be grown between the two.

CRITICISING OTHERS

Long-term, beneficial change doesn't come from criticising others, even if the criticisms are valid. It is significantly aided by being an example of whatever we wish to improve. Focus on the good, not the perceived bad.

BETTER VERSION

When things become challenging, some people turn themselves into enemies. Others use the opportunity to grow into a better version of themselves. When we have an ear for the Divine, we will be guided on how to assist that growth most beneficially.

WHAT WE THINK

We are generally not learning the thing we think we are, and even less, the thing we want. We should be grateful for what makes us grow, even though it may be a love-hate relationship with the things responsible for that growth.

WHERE HAS IT GONE

We seem to have many problems of different sorts. We only have one. We are disconnected from our source. Reconnect and life instantly becomes brighter and lighter. Sometimes, we can't even remember what the problem was.

NO FORCE

Don't try and force people to change. Help them to hear their inner self, and they will inevitably progress.

JEALOUSY

An essential aspect of the spiritual path is understanding the nature of other people's jealousy. Unfortunately, jealousy is rife. The happier and more successful we are, the more we will have to deal with it. Do not underestimate the powerful and negative impact of jealousy. It can come from people you know, people you don't, enemies, and friends. Fortunately, once seen, its power is significantly reduced. The conscious use of our spiritual practices effectively disarms it.

DETRACTORS

When we are focused on what we want to achieve in life, we pay little attention to those who cannot achieve and thereby detract.

SUSPICIOUS AND VICIOUS

The ego, when it is appeased, is still suspicious. When it is alert to danger, it quickly becomes vicious. Neither be that ego nor let other people's viciousness destroy you. The spirit is a robust defence. It gives a shield that makes the insults of the ego meaningless. It provides peace by keeping our eyes not on the ego of others but on their inner being, which is neither suspicious nor vicious. Like us, they belong to the Divine, although they may have difficulty seeing it now.

ALLIANCES

Be careful who you make alliances with. A relationship marked by secretiveness, withholding, flimsy promises, possessiveness, exclusivity, and emotional rollercoaster rides will not benefit you. While you can love a person in this state, they, in return, can neither see nor understand your love. Beneficial relationships are built on happiness, openness, sincerity, peacefulness, and equilibrium. The sunlight glows on everything touched with genuine, simple love.

PLAYING WITH IGNORANCE

It takes maturity and unselfishness to handle the complexities of relationships. Some people, if they do not get what they want, can become a bundle of irrationality and malice, intent on destroying the perceived cause of their pain. They can spend years, decades, and even a lifetime or two blaming any number of people for the injustices they have supposedly endured. Such are the risks of relationships with lesser-evolved people.

DASTARDLY DEEDS IN THE DARK

There is worse karma than that for hatred and viciousness. It is karma for those who are nice to our face but secretly plot our demise. It is worse because its secrecy and manipulativeness make it more destructive. Bad karma will manifest as physical, mental, and energetic problems. Of course, if you would like a beautiful life and good karma, don't be mean. Don't be scheming. And, most of all, don't pretend to be good and plot dastardly deeds in the dark.

DON'T THROW STONES

We should never set ourselves up as the judge of another's character. Far less should we do so based on other people's opinions of that person. Whatever issues we have with someone, we should address with the person themselves in a direct but good-willed way. We are all a work in progress. Don't hold onto the bad. Keep your eyes on the good, but don't miss an opportunity to help someone see something in a better way. Don't let people hurt you, but neither hurt them.

STAGES

Although we have goodwill toward everyone, our responses to people need to be appropriate to the situation. Otherwise, we can be foolish, weak, conciliatory, or naive.

1. If a gentle word works, fantastic.
2. If not, we may need to be more direct.
3. If that doesn't work, distance may be appropriate.

SPACE SAVER

When people we are close to do things that hurt us, we need to try and get the relationship back on track. We can say, "You are hurting me. Is that your intention?" Sometimes, that is enough. If the person is not interested in addressing the underlying issue, we can communicate that we love them but must protect our emotional health. They may reassess their approach if they value the relationship or friendship enough. Space is a good protection if they're not ready or don't care enough to do the necessary emotional work.

NO FAILURE

Don't ever feel that you have a "failed" relationship. Every relationship is a success in that it will be working on the most pivotal and helpful issues for those involved. It may not be working out how you foresaw. It may not be what you want. But trust that it is in everyone's best interest and doing exactly what it is meant to be doing.

GROWTH PROCESSES

Relationships have different purposes and manifest in different forms, with their own timing. Not every relationship is going to be a lifelong, harmonious one. Many are going to be growth processes. The beauty of everyone's freedom is that they have the freedom to learn (or not learn) at their own pace. That may or may not be conducive to the ongoing nature of a good relationship (or one with you).

MENTAL CLIMATE

ENERGETIC CLIMATE

Ordinary people with minimal self-awareness are highly influenced by the mental environment they are subject to. If they are in a hostile energetic climate, it will bring out their nastiness or anxiety. If they are in a positive climate of goodwill and freedom, they will become much nicer people. Thus, leaders must set the mental environment as high as possible and keep it there.

EMOTION POWER

Our emotions are extremely powerful. They are the driving force behind our life decisions. They are more powerful than our minds because whoever fell in love with their mind? Whoever dedicated their entire life to a cause via their intellect? Whoever courageously set out on a life-changing path of discovery without the insistence of their heart? Learn to use the power of your emotions.

TEAM PLAYER

Being a true team player doesn't mean forming a loyal group of people who will work towards your personal cause. It means including everyone (like you would in a large family with many different people) and working for the genuine good of all.

BOSSES AND LOSERS

Life can seem to have two options: be in charge or be the underdog. That is because we interact with life as struggling egos. At a higher level, these concepts don't enter our minds. We respond to life appropriately and do what is needed. If leadership is required, and we are suitably capable, we lead. If it's not, or we are not competent in that area, we don't. Both are fine because we live as happy responders to life, not insecure egos needing constant affirmation of worth.

INCLUSIVITY

Self-oriented people include only those they believe will further their motives and causes. More evolved people understand that inclusivity is the most productive and positive way to be. As such, their endeavours are life-enhancing, successful, and significantly contributory. Truly inclusive people do not gossip, listen to gossip, pull others down, compete for personal power, or try to benefit from someone else's suffering. Their eyes, minds, and talents are directed toward whatever is best for everyone in any given situation.

COMPETITION

Healthy competition is not detrimental to our well-being and progress. It is advantageous. It helps us to recognise the weaker areas within ourselves that need improvement.

COMPARISON AND CAPABILITY

The question is not how you are doing compared to someone else but how you are doing compared to what you are capable of.

SHARING

What we want to make stronger in ourselves will be strengthened by sharing it with others.

> *When we share, we gain.*
> *When we withhold, we lose.*
> *When we give away, we keep.*
> *When we hold tightly, we are left with nothing.*

SIDES

When we see life as part of us and us as part of life, every mistake and every victory is ours. There are no sides. We are part of every side.

FORCE

1. Don't force people. Inspire, encourage, and help them, but let them move under their own steam.

2. Don't force situations. Work with them, contribute to them, and do your best. You don't know everything. Things need to evolve in their own way.
3. Don't force yourself (in body, mind, or spirit). Pay attention, be committed to your well-being, and make the most of your life, but you are part of the universe. Your life is not your sole making.

ADOLESCENT OR FIRING ADULT

If you do not get to the point of truly making your own decisions in life, regardless of what parents, authority figures, mentors, spouse, and family think, you will never truly grow up. You may be forty or seventy, but developmentally, you will always be an adolescent. Perhaps a wonderful and talented one, but you will not be a fully alive, independent, firing adult.

PLAY FAIR

We can ask for things to be fair without imposing one ego over another. It doesn't have to be about whose ego wins. We can keep the focus on what is fair and right for all concerned, including ourselves.

CONFIDENT VULNERABILITY

There is a particular poignant vulnerability to the supremely confident.

LEADERSHIP

To be a genuine leader means dedicating ourselves to our people. We don't use people for our outright or disguised benefit. Most people will intuitively sense our motives (selfish or unselfish), and we will be trusted or not accordingly.

SPECIAL OR ORDINARY

Because the ego is acutely insecure, it is exclusive and desires to be seen as special. Because the spirit is naturally secure, it is inclusive, humble, authentic, and "ordinary" in the best sense of the word.

LOVING FOCUS

In every situation, we should keep our thoughts on the following:

- What can I give to this person?
- What can I give to this group?
- What can I give to this situation?

Such a focus will naturally make our energy field loving, regardless of our personality or what is said or done.

WANTED

A person with an honest intention to love will always be wanted. We may not be wanted where we want to be wanted, but Life will unfailingly want us.

UPDATE YOUR PERSONALITY

Treat your personality as you do your clothes. Your clothes can be changed whenever you want. You can even change your entire wardrobe if you want a brand-new image. Does your choice of clothes make a difference in how people perceive you? Yes, it does. Does your personality make a difference in how people perceive you? Yes, it does. But is it you? No, it is not.

TOUGH LOVE

If you want to be a good leader,
you have to be tough.
Tough enough to weather storms.
Tough enough to weather insults.

Tough enough to look at your own mistakes
way before you look at anyone else's.
Tough enough to care about people
who want to hurt you.

Tough enough to weather
people's right and wrong decisions.
A leader does not have the luxury
of putting themselves first.

A leader does not have the luxury of putting
those they like before those they don't.
Love and leadership are not weak.
They are tough as hell and tender as a baby's kiss.

HEALING

BENEVOLENCE

When we look at people benevolently, we see them as what they are capable of, not what they are necessarily demonstrating right now.

ENTIRELY OURS

What happens inside us is entirely ours. Even though other people and outside energies can affect us, how we manage that is always our choice. That is not a criticism but a great freedom. We are not victims of unwanted influences. We have the power to create our inner selves how we want. If you make a mess, at least acknowledge it is your own mess. That way, one day, you will want to clean it up.

GRIEF

Although the advanced spiritual student becomes less and less prone to grief and incapable of loneliness, they can miss the presence of loved ones they no longer see. The flower blooms and then dies. Its life and beauty are missed and remembered fondly.

ADDING NOT SUBTRACTING

If you are struggling to leave behind some aspect of yourself or your life, don't see it as losing something. See it as adding something to yourself. You are every experience, friendship, and love of every kind that you have ever had. Our life requires constant forward movement, but we are not losing bits of ourselves along the way. We are gathering energy, refining it, and using it for larger, more impactful, and encompassing purposes.

SOLE SOUL

If we are struggling with something we feel has been taken from us (either by someone else's actions, our decision, or the events of life), it is an excellent time to strengthen our resolve to see ourselves as joyous beings by sole (soul) virtue of what is inside us.

MIND THE MIND

Your mental health is crucial. If you find the claws of depression and fear are pulling you into a dark alley, then you need to find a way out. You can do many things to help this process, but all require a conscious decision to do so. Value your happiness. You and your well-being are worth the effort. Definitely, the spiritual path is ideal in the battle against depression and fear because, with time and practice, it eliminates the very basis of both.

BREAKDOWNS, BREAKUPS, AND MAKEUPS

Breakups of all kinds hurt. What is actually breaking up? It is our concept of what the other person is supposed to do or be for us. Instead of thinking of the breakup as a loss, we can see it as an evolution. People have a right to choose how they want to live. That may or may not be in line with us. Either way, life constantly evolves. It involves countless big and little breakdowns for things to be made up, reformed, and reborn.

MAGNIFY

If we look for faults in others, we will undoubtedly find them. However, if we keep our eyes on the beauty and goodness in others, we will magnify it in them and us.

POISON

Some people have a poisonous impact on us. It is not necessarily how they act towards us, which will be determined by social convention, but energetically. Poison primarily stems from jealousy and competitiveness. How do we get the poison out of our system? It's sometimes wise to avoid certain people.

However, energy knows neither time nor space, so that won't necessarily fix the problem. We have to burn up the karma that the other person creates. We burn up the accumulated content of the person in our system. Less appealing but equally important, we must also burn up our own accumulated content. This way, we are left with a clear channel for the Divine to flow.

GIVE IT UP

When I started working with Thomas Hora as a spiritual student, he was firmly focused on forgiveness. I was only twenty-two years old, but already, there seemed much to forgive. We accumulate more and more over the years. Learning what to do with the hurt we collect is important. True forgiveness is not sacrificing ourselves to someone else's nasty, destructive ways. It's something much more effective than that. It is learning how to dismantle the negative impact of blame.

CLEAN IT UP

Setting aside periods for cleansing and healing processes is highly beneficial. You will be amazed at how much stuff you carry around. Forgiveness will always be a critical element of our inner work because most of what we do is burn up karma, our own and other people's.

BURNING UP

When we look at or think of people, we should try to recall the best we have seen in them and delete everything below that. Every evening, before we go to sleep, we should go through the events of the day that hurt or worried us and picture them as being burned up in the fire of compassion and Divine light. This process relieves us of carrying the weight of other people's problems. If we are serious students of life, we will not only burn up the day's bad but also the day's everything so that the next morning is a fresh, clean slate of possibility.

CHAPTER 9

tools for growth

EVERYTHING IS USEFUL

If you want to save yourself a great deal of pain, use your relationships as tools for growth. Every time you find yourself bemoaning something the other person has done, tell yourself that it is helping you become a better version of yourself.

1. If someone is unfaithful, see it as an opportunity to understand that you can never be betrayed by the Love that is always beside you.
2. If someone is angry, see it as an opportunity to learn how to maintain your inner peace no matter the circumstances.
3. If someone is disengaged, see it as an opportunity to increase your engagement with Life.
4. If someone is controlling, see it as an opportunity to strengthen your ability to manage your own life the way you want.

In this way, you will stop blaming people for their shortcomings and use everything to your advantage as a growth opportunity. Life takes care of the rest.

EMOTION

Emotion is a powerful tool. We don't want to get rid of our emotions. We want to use them. Many people find that their emotions rule them rather than the other way around. They are wildly pushed around by them and end up doing and saying regrettable things. Emotion is the charge behind creation. You can learn to direct your emotions into forming projects and life how you want. In this way, even the "bad" emotions can be used to your advantage rather than against you. For example, anger can give some people enough fire to fix up situations that need fixing up. That is a good rather than a destructive use of anger.

COMMUNICATION

Honest and openhearted communication is something you have to keep working on with your partner. Sometimes, ask each other questions that you wouldn't usually ask. Examples of good questions are:

1. What inspired you to want to get to know your partner when you first met them?
2. Is there an area of your life in which you would like your partner to be more involved?
3. What is a memory from your childhood that forms how you see your relationship?
4. What are you most proud of in your partner?

CHAPTER 10

the rise after the fall

THE TROUBLE WITH FALLING IN LOVE

Although highly enjoyable (at certain stages), falling in love is problematic.

1. The first problem is **who** we fall in love with. We can fall in love with anyone: a gay person when we are not gay (or the wrong gender), a married person who is not married to us, an unsuitable person in age, personality, lifestyle, or future goals, or, worst of all, a person who doesn't love us in return. However, even if we fall in love with a gender-appropriate, sexual-orientation-appropriate, availability-appropriate, age-appropriate, life-goals-appropriate person, falling in love is still problematic because of the inherent dynamic of the process itself.
2. This leads to our second problem, the **design** of the falling-in-love mechanism. The mechanism of falling in love is designed to gain something it is

incapable of gaining. It seeks wholeness and safety but inevitably leads to pain, fear, failure, and falling out of the love we fell into.

We need not give up on love, but we do need to understand it.

LOOKING AND NOT FINDING

The nature of human consciousness is to seek completeness.

1. At the **physical level,** it is perceived as joining with another (preferably loved and desired) body. Regardless of the shallow talk and jokes people commonly exchange about sex, most people look for a profound sense of connection and unity in their sexual relationships. Need I tell you about the innumerable problems people have in this pursuit?
2. If the body is fragmented and needs another body to complete itself, the **emotional body** is even more fractured. Finding emotional completeness is about as successful as finding physical completeness.

How can we approach the whole arena of love with a different understanding and, thus, a different outcome?

TIME

Time helps with many things. It helps with infatuations that are going nowhere. For instance, if one falls in love with a person who is involved with someone else, then even the most obsessed person will generally accept their losses and move on after a while. Sometimes, the so-called *loved one* has turned into a God in the mind of the in-love one who has attached their emotional barrenness to that person. The real person and the one in the mind of the love-stricken person become totally unrelated. Usually, however, time will bring about the dissolution of unfulfilled infatuations.

Not only does time dissolve infatuations that go nowhere, but it also dissolves relationships once they are established. The stuff of life, the brokenness of people, the dissatisfaction people feel with what their mate was supposed to be, and the inability of couples to live harmoniously becomes painful enough that many couples break up at this point. Alternatively, they may stay together but live out the rest of their relationship in secret despair or outright rage.

CLIMBING UP

If this sounds rather depressing, we are ready to understand what makes love work. Is there an alternative to abandoning relationships, secret despair, and the stress of conflict? Yes, indeed, there is, but it has little to do with falling in love and much to do with the development of true love. Genuinely loving people are uncommon because love involves a great deal of honesty, introspection, unselfishness, and forgiveness. True love is very different to falling in love, but we mustn't stop the *fall* of falling in love. There's a certain surrender to falling in love. We have to let go of something of ourselves to fall in love with another person. After the fall of falling in love, there is a steep climb back up again, but we can make sure that we are climbing in the right direction. And that makes all the difference.

CHAPTER 11

price of love

DEVOTION

Relationships have a price. It's not that relationships are a sacrifice. After all, who wants a life of sacrifice? It is more a matter of priorities. We can't do everything in life, and we can't be with everyone. We automatically make priorities by choosing what we will do and with whom. If something is at the top of our list, other things must come second, third, or last.

The price of a successful relationship is *devotion*. Devotion is, essentially, commitment to something we value. What are we devoted to? Surely not what another person wants. I think most people would agree that being devoted to that would be problematic even with the best of people. So, what exactly are we devoted to? We are devoted to the well-being of another person. And we are devoted to the well-being of the relationship. We honour the other person's value and the relationship's worth.

We decide that someone else's life is as important to us as our own. This is necessary because endless things in life will pull us in different directions and work against the relationship's stability. No relationship survives or, more accurately, survives happily without a commitment to the genuine happiness of the other person. We do not have to sacrifice our destiny, talents, friendships, or ambitions, but their impact on the other person has to be seriously considered.

When times are uncomfortable, challenging, not what we wanted or imagined, or actively distressing, we should not revert to dishonesty, nondisclosure, or manipulation to get our way. What good is getting our way if that way is destructive to our partner? We will end up suffering anyway from the painful demise of our relationship. A different, new, reformed way can evolve. Some things aren't that important, and disagreement is of minimal importance. Some things have a huge impact on the lives of both people, and some agreement has to be earnestly sought. Compromise is not difficult when the people involved care about the other's emotional, mental, and physical health. Although it seems too obvious to say, there has to be a commitment not to harm the other person. Many people, consciously or unconsciously, view relationships as business partnerships where they try to get the most for the lowest price. That is not even a good business relationship.

I remember listening to a radio conversation with an exasperated wife who complained that her husband did not tell her he loved her. "When we married," said the equally frustrated husband, "I told you I loved you. That stands unchanged until and if such time I tell you that I don't love you!" In his mind, it was black and white. He was committed to the marriage. It was not necessary to keep reaffirming that. Understandably, his answer was not received well by a wife who wanted more emotional intimacy.

TOUCHED BY LOVE

Like gardens, relationships need attention if they are to flourish. If we forget about our garden for long periods, we will find that something other than our design will have taken over the garden beds. They will become full of weeds, which will choke the plants. Maybe some new plants will start growing from seeds that have blown into the garden, taken root, and claimed the garden for themselves. They might even be great-looking plants, but they are not what we intended for our garden. If we love our garden, we must watch over, protect, feed, and water it.

As much as we may love and enjoy someone (or, at least, for a reasonable amount of the time), relationships are primarily a responsibility. Often, people talk about a new baby as a gift given to the parents, as if the child is for their pleasure. Of course, children are a gift. However, looking at my three newborns, I never felt they were even remotely here for my benefit. On the contrary, I looked at each one and felt the great responsibility of a tiny, totally dependent human. My task was to keep their little bodies, minds, and souls safe. I was acutely aware of the effect of everything negative on the forming consciousness of children. I frequently looked at parents and wondered if they realised how their words and actions affected their children. Yes, indeed, it seemed to me an almighty responsibility.

If we don't want to be responsible for another life (tiny or adult), it is better to abstain from the commitment. Otherwise, we will end up hurting the other person, ourselves, and numerous others along the way. Falling in love is relatively easy. All we need is an open heart, the ability to see good in someone else, and a willingness to engage intimately with another being. Falling in love versus committed love is as different as feeling that a baby is here for our benefit versus embarking on the long, conscientious responsibility of raising a beautiful, well-adjusted human. A partner is not a newborn (thank God), and we can expect much more reciprocity. Nevertheless, the commitment to hold another's life as important as or more important than our own is the same.

CHAPTER 12

can you love too much?

It has become somewhat fashionable in the self-development realm for people (especially women) to proclaim that their problem is that they "love too much and have to learn how to let other people love them". Everything about that is incorrect and ultimately unhelpful. You cannot love too much. Genuine love does not come from your limited and tire-able self but from Source.

People who feel that they "love too much" unconsciously believe that the best way to get what they want (be it support, success, security, sex, money, safety, or care) is to be "loving". "Generosity" in specific aspects of life is used to try and balance the scales and get a valued return. It is neither true love nor true generosity. It is an unacknowledged agreement. It is ultimately exhausting and does not work (or works minimally and begrudgingly). Seeing the motive behind this sort of "love" takes honesty and is, indeed, embarrassing. But what is not seen cannot be healed or transcended. If you want to be genuinely loving, there is no other way.

If you ask those around the people who say that they "give too much" if that is how they see them, most will say no. We knowingly or unknowingly sense when something is offered with strings. On the other hand, someone who lives from an energy field of love is usually perceived as loving regardless of what they do, don't do, say, or don't say. It's not about doing and saying. It's about energy field and consciousness. The energy field of love speaks for itself.

True *generosity* does not want something in return, so it does not get frustrated and tired. True *love* does not want something in return, so it does not become hurt and withdraw its love. It does not evaluate the scales of what has been given and taken and decide that not enough is coming back. It is inexhaustible. Every time you get into the sphere of genuine love, it is a reward, not a drain. First and foremost, love blesses the person who is in the loving consciousness.

CHAPTER 13

the bigger person
FORGIVENESS

Most people consider forgiveness onerous because they think it involves forgiving someone who did something terrible. They think that even though they did it, they will be "the bigger person" and let it go. It doesn't really work.

Humans are made of a trillion different memories, both good and bad (predominantly bad), remembered and forgotten (mostly forgotten). The memories are stuck fast as a thick mass in the energy system. They come out in the body, mind, and life experience.

As we evolve, the stuck mass of memories starts to dissolve, usually slowly but sometimes quickly. The memory mass loosens, things get released, and we see life differently. We start to understand people and why they do the things they do. We begin to realise that everyone is innocent in the sense that if they knew better, they would do better. People don't know what they're doing. That is what we call forgiveness, or, really, it's simply the way of evolution. Evolution is always moving towards what makes us free and light—no mess, no stuck mass, no mass of memory—free and light.

CHAPTER 14

right on cue

One morning in a coffee shop, the manager growled several derogatory and unwarranted demands at the staff member beside her. The staff member was a young, inexperienced girl. She looked defeated. She had probably had too many similar remarks thrown her way that day.

To protect the girl, I wanted to say to the manager, *You are being mean.*

I opened my mouth and said, "You are..."

But then I stopped. I saw in the manager's eyes frustration and anxiety.

I changed my tone and continued quietly, "You are... very stressed."

The manager's look softened, and she started to laugh. I laughed, too, and then others around us joined in.

"I have had a bad morning," said the manager.

Her whole demeanour changed. Before I left, she approached me and offered me a free coffee card.

"Your coffee was late," she said by way of explanation.

My coffee wasn't late. The timely idea of a compassionate response, instead of a reactive one, made everything right on cue.

CHAPTER 15
thanks love

It was Anzac Day. In Australia, that is when servicemen and women are remembered and honoured. It is also when the shops don't open till 1 p.m. As it's a once-a-year phenomenon, people often forget. Along with a growing collection of citizens, I stood outside the local supermarket, waiting for it to open. The local homeless man sat next to the entrance, ready for donations. He probably wasn't exactly homeless, but I can't call him a beggar because he was too polite and dignified.

"Got a few spare coins, love?" he always asked.

If you say no, he doesn't object.

If you give him something, he invariably says, "Thanks, love."

I was at the head of the supermarket line.

When I first approached the unopening automatic doors, the man said, "Not open for fifteen more minutes. Anzac Day, love."

I noticed that he gave other people the same response, but not everyone. Some people he said nothing to.

An equally scruffy man arrived as a shopper. He was probably sixty but, like the homeless man, wore the scars of a hard sixty years. He seemed to know the homeless man and chatted with him after being told about the supermarket's closure.

The shopper looked at the homeless man and said, "So, when are you open, mate?"

Without hesitation, the homeless man replied, "24/7. I'm always open."

"You're keen," said his shopping friend.

Neither changed tone nor cracked a smile, but both had cracked a joke and shared it with all listening.

After a pause, the homeless man turned to me and said, "Got much to buy today, love?"

"Not much," I answered with a smile.

"What's on your list?" he asked.

"I'll tell you," I said, pulling my list out with a dramatic flurry.

I was pretty sure that he didn't really want me to read through my boring list.

"Butter," I said, pausing to see if that was enough.

He nodded encouragingly to go on.

"Eggs," I continued with another pause.

"Yes," he said with great interest as if I was reading him the most enthralling story.

By now, everyone else was also listening to my shopping list.

"Chocolate," I said with an enthusiastic wave of my arms.

That one was greeted with much approval.

At the end of my list reading, the shopping mate said to the homeless man, "All I heard was chocolate."

We all parted company when the door opened. A man I didn't recognise passed me near the eggs and smiled, acknowledging the pre-shopping exchange.

On my way out of the supermarket, I gave the homeless man the chocolate I had bought and a little cash.

"Thanks, love," he said, putting the money in his dirty plastic bag. He looked at the chocolate and repeated, "Thanks, love. Thanks a lot."

CHAPTER 16

karma and the beggar

I was at a car wash when a man came up and asked me for 10 cents for the machine. It was one of those car wash places that recognised neither rich nor poor. You had to have exactly the right coins, or it wouldn't work. It didn't take credit cards. It did have a change machine, but it was as fussy as the car wash machine and often didn't work properly.

The man looked stressed and said that he was late, that the change machine wouldn't take his money, and that all he needed was 10c more. I gave him a coin, and off he went. A minute later, he was back asking, like an apologetic beggar, to borrow a dollar because "the damn thing wants another dollar!" I gave it to him.

As I finished washing my car, a beautiful, new, black Mercedes pulled up next to me, and the window went down. There was the man, far from beggar-mode.

He handed me his business card and said, "I run a car hire company. If you need a car, you can call me."

With many thank-yous, he drove off waving.

That was good value for a dollar, I thought.

CHAPTER 17

conscious use

Social media can ignite a feeling of inadequacy in people. Everyone is more gorgeous, has happier relationships, more friends, more accomplished careers, more talented children, and all-around more extraordinary lives. More of more! In reality, the average person is fortunate to have a few of these things for a fleeting moment. People believe others would ridicule them if they knew what they were really like, so most people pretend. Pretension breeds duplicity. It means we will say and act one way, but in a million other ways, we will convey a different message.

I remember looking at the social media page of a person I knew well. It was full of adoration for his wife and children. They were a gorgeous-looking family. It was most impressive. However, I knew the man had ambivalent feelings about his wife and an eye for love interests outside the family. So, to me, the whole thing seemed silly, although common enough. He did not mean to hurt anyone or intentionally deceive, although he did both. Like most people, he was struggling to find his happiness. It would have seemed like the best available option to him. Isn't this typical of human nature, in one form or another?

Social media mirrors human nature—no worse, no better. Some people divorce it to get rid of one such problem. One could also choose to use it consciously. If we talk consciously in face-to-face life, we'll use social media consciously. That's all social media is—talking, be it:

- superficial or deep
- depressing or jollying
- fear-mongering or sensible
- divisive or healing
- blabbing or listening
- making fun of others or having fun with life
- always wanting something or always giving something
- sneaking or accounted for
- self-oriented or all-oriented

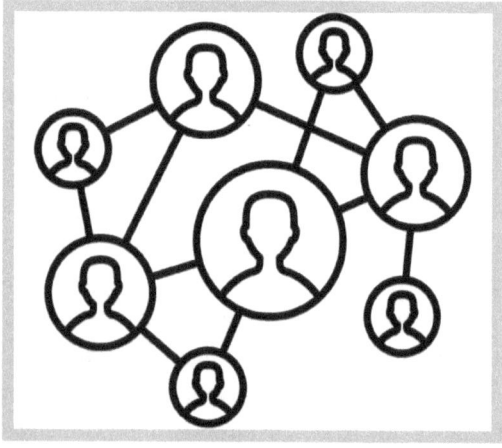

CHAPTER 18

Enemies

QUESTION AND ANSWER

- *Question:* I have a troubling situation with betrayal, gossip, and malicious plotting, all while smiling directly into my face. How should I respond to someone who appears to be nice and likes to small talk with me but is a liar? I don't think it is a good idea to let her know that I can see what is happening, but I also don't think it makes sense to appear like nothing is happening.
- *Answer:* People are commonly just as you describe. It is an opportunity to focus on lifting your consciousness into a higher space. This is the usual thing people do out of ignorance, and it is all ego-driven. As you say, if you honestly tell the person what you can see them doing, it will only make it worse as people do not want to see their shortcomings. We must practise compassion. Our role in life is to develop to the point where we are not affected by such things. We see it, and then we forgive it because we understand the weakness in

the person. We maintain a peaceful equilibrium and spread the love we feel in our soul.
- *Question:* What is an intelligent way "to spread the love we feel in our soul"? Saying meaningful things is not allowed by the person, or it doesn't help. I feel that small talk is like filling a space with empty words. I am mostly quiet and go on my way, but some people do not accept that. The atmosphere is a disturbed one. What would be a good way to deal with it—a way that we are true to ourselves and the other one?
- *Answer*: I think one must be responsive daily to what is wisest with any given person. As you say, the peace inside is first. After that, what is wisest to do or say may vary depending on the receptivity or negativity of the other person. I listen to my feelings after seeing such a person. If I feel bad, I assume there is a lot of ill will from the person, and I protect myself as best I can. That can change with time. If I cannot escape the person, I ask God to help me stay safe. I also try to release the anger inside myself about other people's malice. It can take a while. If we keep working on it, it does go.
- *Question:* I need to work on releasing the anger inside. I did say one stupid thing that I regretted. Interestingly, people keep that in mind instead of all the good things I have done. When one works on seeing everything and everyone with a compassionate eye, one can happily be compassionate to oneself.
- *Answer:* Absolutely. We forgive ourselves, too. Besides, sometimes, it is appropriate to express anger. However, an enemy will look for any little

thing to grab onto, so we must be aware of that. If they can't find anything to grab onto, they will often make something up!

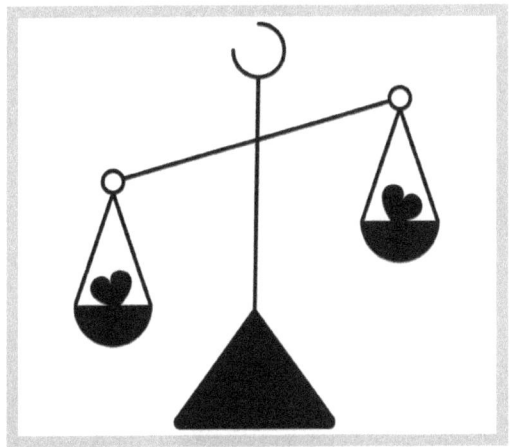

CHAPTER 19
another chance: bethany and daniel

STORY

It was Daniel and Bethany's time. It was a gift from life, or perhaps it was life's little joke to itself. Dan and Beth were not laughing. It was too promising.

Dan turned to Beth and said, "If I asked you to marry me, would you say yes?"

Beth was surprised. It was such a serious question. Daniel's eyes would not let hers turn away. They were demanding, *Answer me, now.*

Before her mind could formulate some reasonable concerns, even objections, a smile jumped into the arena and smoothed itself over Beth's mouth. The deal was sealed in the passing of a few seconds. For the shortest breathing space, Dan and Beth relaxed. The moment was so innocent that both felt naked and embarrassed. Perhaps too much of themselves had been shown to the other. It was a marriage proposal that would go horribly wrong.

In retrospect, the signs were clear, but Beth didn't want to believe them. The coming months became more confusing until she could not remember if Dan even vaguely liked her. One final day, he casually told her he had recently met up with an old friend. They had reignited their friendship. He was going to move to her city and live with her. Beth was incredulous. Daniel decided that the best approach was to act like there was no reason why Beth would be anything but happy about his new adventure. This brought the fire out in Bethany.

How dare he hurt me like that, she fumed to herself. *How dare he ask for my love and trust and then disregard it as if it never happened.*

Dan was much bigger than Beth, but she hit him. He seethed with fury because he could not hit back. They both stared at each other like the world was about to explode. At least it was an even match. Seeing that Dan meant to carry through with his plan and do so without remorse, Beth threw herself towards the door.

After a while, the anger faded, but something worse took its place—grief. Every morning, following the heels of waking consciousness, Beth would hear, *It's over. Accept it. How many times must one release the same person?* A thousand times, she scolded herself, *Why did you give him your heart? You knew it was a terrible idea.* But she did give him her heart. It was already done. Once the contract is signed, it can only be nullified by a painful untangling. Beth wondered how Dan was doing in his new relationship. She felt that he must have adjusted by now. He must be happy. It was his decision, after all.

Sometimes, Beth dreamed of a mysterious friend. The friend had many disguises, but she always recognised her friend by their advice and energy field.

"If you didn't give Daniel your heart," said the friend, "he could not heal. It's the price you paid for his healing."

Beth wondered if the price was worth it. Maybe it was all for naught anyway.

"Will I see him again?" asked Beth.

"Yes, you will see him," replied the friend. "He never went to live with the girl. He didn't even start the relationship. There was no need for it once you left. He didn't love her but needed a reason to make you leave. If one cannot trust that one will be loved even at one's worst, the healing cannot begin. One will always be lying about what is inside oneself."

"Will he heal?" asked Bethany.

"That, my dear, is the enthralling story of life," said the friend. "For now, it is enough for you to know that love is its own reward."

Five years later, Bethany was looking at a rundown cottage. It was perfect. For some reason, Dan seemed to think otherwise as he looked suspiciously at the wildly creaking floorboards. Beth was too busy to notice as she gazed with mounting excitement at the ceiling, which contained an array of house spiders and other insects happily living their communal lives.

Dan glanced sideways at the real estate agent of the village as if to say, *Why in God's name did you bring us here? It's a disaster.* The real estate agent couldn't help but have an apologetic look. He was of the same ilk as Dan.

When Bethany was a child, her family often set out on the five-hour drive to their relative's farm. Although she never mentioned it to anyone, she had a game that she played. Her favourite houses on the way were the rundown ones with rusty roofs, tall grass, and broken fences. For each forgotten cottage, she dreamed about how she would fix it up. She imagined living there and making progress with the restoration of her charge. She thought about the sweeping, painting, rubbish removal, and gardening. She knew that, given a chance, her charges would turn into beautiful, loving, and loved homes.

Bethany turned brightly to Dan and held his arm, "Can you feel it? It's wonderful."

"No," he said emphatically. "I can't feel anything except disgust. The plaster is falling off the walls. The roof is leaking. God only knows how much asbestos is lying around the house. There are rat droppings everywhere. The garden is full of rubbish. I hate it."

To ensure Bethany was certain of his position on the matter, he stared into her eyes and repeated firmly, "Bethany, no. It's horrible. Let's go."

The agent looked awkward. Bethany glanced through the dirty, broken window and spotted a rose flowering beneath a dense blackberry bush. A little bird bobbed its head.

Dan tried being conciliatory and said, "Come on, Beth. This house is only fit for the bulldozer. Let's look at all the other houses the agent has lined up for us. We will find some other place that you will love even more."

It was a sensible suggestion if only Beth could bring herself to believe it. They spent the afternoon driving around. As they pulled up outside the houses, she made a conscientious effort not to look completely disinterested. She felt that the original cottage was the most beautiful in the village. She almost felt sorry for the other residents of the town. However, her pity was unnecessary because no one else seemed to think the same way. They preferred their large, fabulous houses.

After some months, the rundown cottage was so cheap and everything else so expensive that Dan took a deep breath, wondered why he agreed, and they bought the little house. As much as Dan resented the broken and fragile state of the cottage, he also secretly hoped it could be saved. Soon, it became one of the loveliest cottages in the village. Although it wasn't an instant love affair for Dan, he grew to love it. He felt happy and relaxed there. Every little improvement reassured him that healing is not only possible but inevitable. As for Bethany, she loved it from when she was a young child looking out the window of their family car, watching the passing paddocks dotted with neglected homes that needed another chance.

CHAPTER 20

wild beast spirit: dahlia and the shepherd

STORY

Dahlia could be a formidable foe when fighting for someone she loved, for the protection of someone's soul, or for something worth fighting for. However, by nature, she was a gentle soul. The fighting spirit only seemed to enter her when she fought for something other than herself. Then, a different force entered her. That force tended not to give in until it had fulfilled its mission. As quickly as it appeared, it seemed to retreat to where it came from until some commanding power directed it to return.

For many years, Dahlia found the presence of a German shepherd in the house very reassuring. It gave a sense of balance for most of the time when the warrior spirit was elsewhere. However, German shepherds bring their own problems. Instinctively dominant and suspicious, they defend first and ask questions later. They are intensely alert, observant, and intelligent. They live to serve as protectors. Of course, these instinctive tendencies must be modified by strict training, or they will take charge of everything and start ruling the world. Given that they are dogs, most of us would prefer that our house is run by relatively civilised human rules rather than dog pack behaviour.

At 50 kilos, Dahlia was a slight thing and would probably have needed another 20 kilos to match her shepherd's strength. When she was walking her dog, it became a mind game. Shepherds are not only highly protective of their whole pack but will tend to pick the one person they must protect above all else. When away from this person, they can refuse to eat, get depressed, and wait for their world to be right again.

When Dahlia walked her shepherd, he looked suspiciously at every cute, white, fluff-ball dog as if it was a possible threat to Dahlia's life. The walks were a matter of her continuously insisting that she was in charge and that they would do it her way. In his mind, he could have it all sorted out so very quickly. Everything comes at a price. Dahlia paid for the comfort of her shepherd's protectiveness by having to contain his *wild beast* spirit so that there were no casualties.

PART THREE

spiritual path

ENTIRELY SELFISH

CHAPTER 21

Spotlights

SPIRITUAL PATH

LIFE PURPOSE

PURPOSE

We must strengthen, expand, and extend all the energetic systems of our being. It takes inner work and commitment. We must work with every level of our being to make it more harmonious, in tune, efficient, and effective. That is the purpose of life.

LIGHTS ON

Follow what lights you up, even if it is only a small glow. Throw yourself into it, but don't demand how it must be. Let life lead you. The most important thing you have to give is your wholehearted energy. And if your light leads you on a different path, then take it with absolute trust.

MADE BY YOU

Remember that your misery is made by you. This is great news because if it is made by you, then you can unmake it. Be determined to consciously create a peaceful mind and a healthy body. The world can throw many things at us, and everything we try to do does not work out. But everything we determine to do in our mind will surely work out exactly as we have scripted. You are blessed beyond your wildest imagination. Take a little of that blessing and make it live wholeheartedly in you.

NO MISTAKE

Nothing that you sincerely want to do is a mistake. Remind yourself that there are beings around you who are there to help. Open yourself every day so that you can hear what they're telling you. Be a completely open channel.

ABSOLUTE

Be devoted to something good—anything good. Dedicating yourself to anything positive will transform you, your life, and your environment.

STORY OF YOUR LIFE

Turn your life into a good story. Resolve to make the very most out of yourself.

WHO'S WORKING FOR WHO?

We should each decide, preferably as young adults, how much money will be enough for our needs, responsibilities, and what we want to do in this lifetime. Money and standard of living are highly subjective and seductive (particularly in wealthier countries). We can reach the end of our life and realise that we spent it all making money to live the life we were supposed to live but never quite got to do. Make your approach to money and livelihood work for you, not the other way around.

THE QUESTION

The question is not how am I doing compared to other people, but how am I doing compared to myself? We all have different energy imprints, strengths, and challenges. On the spiritual path, it's similarly important not to compare ourselves with people who are further ahead of us. A grand garden may have a couple of magnificent trees, but what would it be if that was all it had? It needs the grass, bushes, bulbs, and flowering plants. It needs a vast array of different species, big and small, plain and spectacular, short-lived and long-lived, to make it a beautiful place.

BLOOMING

Fulfilment on the path of personal growth does not mean becoming more like someone we admire. It means becoming a more fully flowering version of ourselves.

HAPPY GAME

Whether life blesses us or torments us, plays with us or abuses us, kisses us or destroys us is our choice. Choose to be blessed and kissed and you will be part of a happy game.

UPGRADE REQUIRED

When you are struggling with confidence in one situation in your life, think of a situation where you feel very confident and calm and where everything works out well. It will become clearer to you what you need to do to make the worse situation better. Sometimes, it means leaving it behind. Sometimes, it means upgrading yourself to a better version of yourself.

BEST BARGAIN

Everything in life has a price. The trouble is that most people pay dearly for worthless things. On the path of wisdom, we still have to pay at various stages, but as soon as we do, we realise that nothing of any value was taken from us. Indeed, everything is given to us. There's no better bargain.

CONNECTED

Despite any indication to the contrary, you can never be disconnected from the invisible, irrevocable, ever-present connections of Love. You are loved. You are here for a purpose. Your life is unique, meaningful, and irreplaceable.

IGNORANCE AND ARROGANCE

Ignorance and arrogance are unfortunate but common bedmates.

OURS TO ANSWER

We only have to answer what is ours to answer.

NOT THIS OR THAT

I am not my body.
I am not my mind.
I am not my relationships.
I am happy and well.
I am here for a purpose.
I will flourish.

MYSTICISM

COMMON MYSTICISM

Mysticism is only mysterious when we don't understand the world beyond the physical. When we understand, it's not mysterious. It is common sense. Perhaps not common to everyone, but common to those on the spiritual path.

SIMPLICITY

Truth is not complicated. The intellect is complicated, but we will never gain our freedom through the intellect.

ALONE

The spiritual path can be scary for many people because you have to walk it alone. You don't have to be without people in your life. You can be married and part of highly interactive groups. However, such relationships are arrangements that are significantly based on need. Nothing wrong with that. That is how healthy relationships form—by satisfying at least a reasonable amount of our needs in a viable and maintainable way. If you are fortunate, those arrangements will be blessed and beneficial. We mustn't confuse the spiritual, inner domain with the external, worldly domain. Both are important. However, if you are ready to develop yourself at a different level, you must get used to being alone. Give yourself periods of solitude. How else can you learn to be comfortable and thrive on the spiritual path?

GATHERING OURSELVES

Many things happen in our communities, families, work, and world. We have little choice about much of it, but we have total choice about what is inside us. Happiness develops within our being, not from outside influences. It is crucial to have time alone to develop this inner awareness of happiness and stability—a few minutes, an hour, a day, a week. We are not gathering more of the world in that space but gathering ourselves into a clear, calm, loving being capable of doing much.

GENTLE WAY

Remember that the spiritual path is generally gentle. The changes in you may seem unnoticeable, but with time, you will radiate love and glow with the power of your spiritual inheritance.

SINKING AND SPRINGING

Growth is formed in the hidden deep. Below the surface, everything can be made into food for the push upwards. The springing forth comes from the sinking deep. The flowering comes from the mess from which it is birthed.

UNCOMFORTABLE

When drawn to a spiritual teacher, one automatically benefits from their energetic field. Don't pick someone you feel comfortable with. Comfort comes from sameness. You will never get anywhere if the teacher knows only what you know. Pick someone who has enough difference and unknowableness to make you UNcomfortable. Then, you're on the path of learning, progress, and change. Yes, there has to be a feeling of being drawn, symmetry, and affection. But without the sense that this could go either way, without risk, nothing of real substance can bounce into existence.

SAFE PLACE

When things are not going well, it is a good time to withdraw into a safe place and drop a layer of our being. Traditionally, that is what ashrams and monasteries are for—a supported environment where it is safe to go within, explore oneself, and shed some negative karma and thought processes. We can make our own safe place. We can learn how to protect ourselves from negative thinking, harmful people, and counter-productive environments. We can align with whatever will help us to create less suffering. We will become cleaner, brighter, and more willing to take up the endless possibilities of life.

COMFORT

Spiritual truth is ultimately comforting. Most people are deeply uncomfortable in life. They will find comfort and freedom if they allow themselves to be led along the spiritual path.

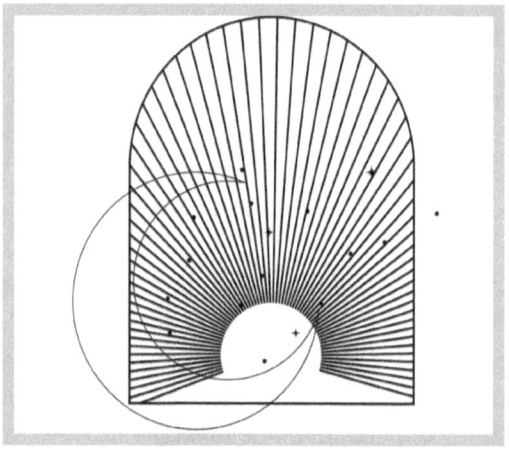

WHO WALKS BESIDE US

When we remember who walks beside us, everything we touch, gaze upon, and turn our attention to has the inner light of creation. Nothing we do can fail in that light of that love and grace.

GRACE

Grace is a gentle thing. It is easily destroyed by selfishness, envy, ill will, and fear. It is easily invited by kindness, hope, forgiveness, and love.

ATTENTION

God does not need our love to be complete. However, when we do not communicate with the Divine or are too busy with our problems and don't trust that the Creator is there, the channels to God are blocked and creation is incomplete. The more attentive we are, the more God seems to pay attention to us.

INSIDE OUT

We must become firmly established within ourselves, and then we can move out into the world. If we try to establish ourselves from the outside with career, achievements, and relationships, we will feel that we are constantly chasing life. It will not end well. Many people start with a passion for something, and they end up feeling like it is draining the life out of them. Every day, we need to meet ourselves on the inside. It is an entirely private matter. There is no one to impress, no one to applaud. Neither is there anyone to disapprove. Who do we meet? Our higher self, our better self, the self who knows why we are here. Whatever we create from the inside will carry unshakeable and positive energy above and beyond our own doing.

CHANGE

It's not the world that needs changing. It's us.

WAVES OF GROWTH

Growth happens in curves or waves ascending upwards. It's not a straight line. In fact, you need the down bends to solidify specific learned processes into your system. That requires you to temporarily lower your vibration from a previous high. Do not see it as a loss but an adjustment. Be assured that once you are on a growth path, there is only one way, and that is up. Don't give too much attention to the downtimes, and you'll bounce out of them relatively quickly onto new heights.

EXPANDING AND CONTRACTING

When we are happy, our instinct is to expand. When we are afraid, our instinct is to contract. In the contractions, find the thread of courage that leads you back to the right sort of expansion.

ABSENCE AND PRESENCE

Without humility, we can never know life's subtler, tender things. We may know success, power, money, control, and social and professional standing. But we will not know love, compassion, the look of peace in another's eyes, or the collapse of self when watching the profound dignity of the ocean. These things require our absence as an ego and our presence as pure energy.

PURITY

Devotion makes everything and everyone beautiful. The purity of devotion brings out the inner beauty of all.

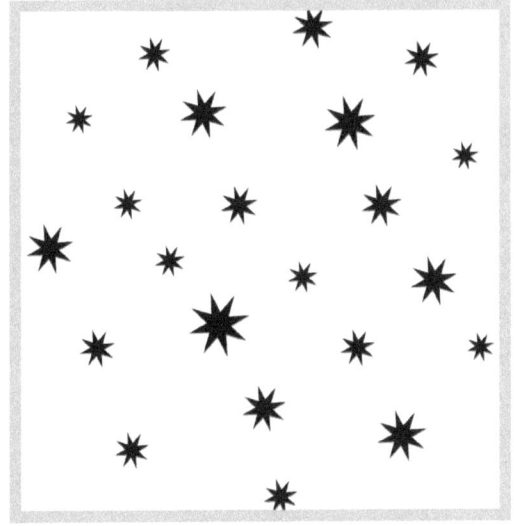

SACRED

Make a sacred space out of your body, mind, and spirit. Refine it every day with whatever practices work best for you. Don't ignore one aspect of your being out of laziness, ignorance, resentment or resistance.

WOO-WOO

I have little tolerance for woo-woo sort of spiritual people who imagine their specialness and quite loudly proclaim it. Yet, invariably, if you look at their lives, they are failing on many levels—relationships, finance, professional success, and mental stability. They are usually emotionally insecure and often mentally unstable. Give me a sane, clear, motivated, intense, "unspiritual" person any day. The spiritual path is not woo-woo. It is realistic and practical. It's just that it deals with different dimensions. One must know what is in those dimensions to know what is realistic and practical there.

SENSE

Having other senses doesn't negate common sense. They belong to different dimensions. We use what is wisest and most appropriate in the situation.

ENLARGED BORDERS

There are many paths to God. Some never mention God. No matter. What matters is that the path leads to increased mental clarity, emotional freedom, physical wholeness, and energetic vibrancy. It matters that we know what we are supposed to do and with whom. It matters that our sense of responsibility expands beyond ourselves, our immediate loved ones, and our communities into the whole of humanity.

JOIN THE DANCE OF LIFE

PARTNERSHIP

When you feel anxious and stressed, remind yourself that while life requires your best effort, courage, and commitment, it functions beautifully of its own accord. Join the dance. Don't sit it out. Trust the music. Do your part, and it will be a happy, successful partnership.

FOCUS

Don't focus on what the world is doing to you. Focus on what you are doing for the world. This simple practice will turn your life from one of fear and anger to one of love and happiness.

WILLING TO SHARE

If we are willing to share—people, money, talents, the limelight, kind-heartedness—we will, one way or another, always have what we need. If we try to own people, hold onto money, hog the limelight, are too scared to express our talents, or are stingy with our love, then life will have a hard time giving us much more than sorrow.

PEACE OR PARTICIPATION

If we only seek peace and security in our lives, our world will become smaller and smaller, and we will become less and less active participants. Serenity is important, but so is involving ourselves in life. Engaging with people and projects inevitably means problems, but the successes and stressors bring new lifeblood into our bodies and spirits. Peace is not our only goal. In a way most aligned with our individual preferences, participation is life-giving.

TRANSMIT PEACE

There is no greater gift than the heart that can transmit peace. By sharing it, we keep it.

CLEAR AND LIGHT

Be helpful without being condescending. The egoic mind condescends because it is insecure. The spirit focuses on sharing whatever will make things joyful, clear, and light.

MADE STRONGER

Wherever you are with your growth, share that with the world in ways that are natural and enjoyable to you. Everything we share is made more robust in our being.

GETTING BIGGER

We need to expand ourselves. Get bigger. Not body-bigger, but the light-that-radiates-from-within bigger. The healthier and more harmonious our being is on the different levels—physical, mental, emotional, and energetic—the greater will be the light that radiates from us. We will become more impactful, beneficial, and creative with less effort. Less effort, but a more effective intention of effort.

CREATIVE PROCESS

Although intense focus is one way of manifesting desires, there is another. We can allow desires to rise, see them as already fulfilled, and then release them into the flow of life. This not only works effectively but also increases our trust that what is important to us is also important to the Creative Process.

PROGRESS AND PRACTICE

STOP TALKING

If you would like a simple practice that is 100% guaranteed to change you for the better—stop talking. If that is too difficult, then cut your talking down by half. The idea is to become conscious of what you say and why. This practice, which I intuitively did for some years at age twenty-two, is transforming. Once you are aware of your talking and it has lost all its compulsiveness, you will be free to talk as much as you want. You won't be so eager to speak anymore.

PRUNING

Where our focus is, so too is our development. When a plant is pruned, its inner eye is on the area that has been cut. It puts all its energy into that part of itself. Thus, a pruned plant will produce abundant growth where it has been pruned.

LIFE CHANGING

When we face big decisions or life changes that worry or scare us, we can tell ourselves, "This will be a life-changing time for me in terms of learning, growth, and opportunity. Whichever way it turns out, I will be better and richer for it."

HESITATION

Life travels along regardless of whether we hesitate or not. Many things change in life for all of us. Every day, every year, is important and different.

LOOKING AND CHANGING

There is always another way of looking at things. All change begins with the realisation that things can be different. Without that concept, the seed of change will not be nourished.

GETTING GOOD

No matter what happens in life and what difficulties you face, treat everything as something that will benefit you in some way. It may be that it's important for you to learn something from the situation. It may be that you will be blessed by the misfortune in some unforeseen way. So long as you approach everything that happens with a positive mindset, you will only get good from it. You'll always be a winner and never a loser. You will carry no suffering, no bad karma, and no regrets.

CHALLENGE

The job of someone who helps us grow is not only to love but to challenge. The presence of such a person will often "irritate" the energy and belief systems of those in contact with them. It is a matter of timing as to when the recipient will realise that the challenge is for their benefit, not for their detriment.

DEPRESSION

Doctors, counsellors, and psychologists effectively help many people with depression. However, if it is an existential depression—a crisis of life-vision, meaning, and purpose—then spiritual teachers are needed. The teacher needs to be the right one for you. Trust your instincts and interests. A living one is great but not necessary. You can access the words of most teachers through their books and recordings. More importantly, you can access their energy field and help simply by asking and being open to receiving it.

SEPARATION

Our problems seem many and infinitely varied. They are not even resolved before new ones arise. No one could solve or foresee them all. Fortunately, they all stem from the same tree and can be handled with one fix. They grow from the tree of separation. If we plant ourselves securely in the right soil, our problems will be seen differently and often disappear. What is the right soil? It cannot be taught. It is felt. It is intuitively understood. Eventually, it is the only way of seeing that makes any sense.

THIS MOMENT

If we accept life as it is, at this moment; people as they are, at this moment; situations as they are, at this moment, we only have to endure the bad things once. Otherwise, we constantly rerun painful experiences and experience them a thousand times over in our minds. Acceptance helps us to think clearly and calmly, giving us more ability to change situations for the better.

AWARE NOT BEWARE

> *Walk safely, knowing who walks with you.*
> *But do not be reckless.*
> *Be aware of everything.*
> *But don't beware of anything.*

ABSORB

If you cannot delete a problem, then absorb it into yourself. It will disappear via a different route.

GOING WITH THE FLOW

If we are awake, we can safely and happily go with the flow, but if we are asleep, the flow can easily lead us into a nightmare.

LIGHT LOAD

The spiritual path is not a burden when it significantly improves our lives. My yoke is easy *and my burden is light (Bible)*.

LIFE EXPERIENCE

If we want our life experience to improve, we mustn't focus on how to get people to like us better, appreciate us more, or give us more of what we want. We must focus on turning ourselves into more loving beings and using as much of our potential as possible in this lifetime.

STRUGGLE

We struggle to find peace within ourselves and with each other, but all the struggle disappears in those moments of acceptance, trust, and love. It disappears into nothingness as if it was all totally unnecessary. Yet, without the struggle, we could not have known the choice.

START THE DAY

Start the day right by talking to your best friend—the Divine. Better still, don't talk. Listen. Be together. That way, your Friend has the most opportunity to reclaim your consciousness so that your day will be maximally happy and least karmic-gathering. A moment of true togetherness will wipe out all your hurts, worries, and fears. That moment will join with many other moments, and your life will be one of grace.

LIGHT WORK

Acceptance makes light work of many a worry.

CHOOSE HAPPINESS

We can choose to be happy. We do not have to accept the bonds that feed sadness. We can choose to be free. We do not have to bow before those who smile with poison on their lips. We can choose life and peace. Happiness is not an accident. It is a deliberate decision. Someone else cannot choose it for us. We must choose it for ourselves. We must align our lives with what we genuinely value.

SIGHT

If we can see the little things, we can see the entire universe.

CREATING GOODNESS

If we insist that life be a certain way, we will create suffering for ourselves. Alternatively, if we start from the simple premise of being happy to be alive and grateful for the good that comes our way, we will be both good and happy.

DECISIONS

Today, I make no decisions by myself. I trust the power that formed me to lead me on the best path for my personal peace and happiness. I do not have to worry about anything.

BEING SOMEBODY

The nature of our ego is to try and turn every situation, conversation, and interaction into something that benefits itself. Without conscious discipline, we are far more selfish and uncaring than we acknowledge. This is not an indictment or an accusation. It is simply the way it is. When we become more aware of the beauty within us and our place in this incredible, miraculous life, our attention is pulled away from building up our egos in an ineffective and pathetic attempt to be somebody. We are already everything we could ever wish to be.

BREATHING

> *Prayer is like breathing.*
> *Always there.*
> *Life-giving.*
> *Healing.*
> *Revitalising.*
> *Stabilising.*
> *Connecting us to the Source.*

MEDITATION

Meditation is not new-age mumbo-jumbo for ungrounded people. True meditation is intelligent, humble, and powerful. It means becoming consciously alive and well. It heals our body, clears our mind, and frees our spirit. In this way, we reduce (and often eliminate) our problems and have the deep satisfaction of living in an ever-evolving, connected, and creative way.

SAFE TRAVELS

We must learn to be the driver of our own life. How many people consciously and deliberately create an extraordinary life? Not many. Most are scared, angry, hopelessly hanging on, or grin-and-bear-it passengers in the vehicle of life, which seems to be driven by someone other than themselves. Jump into the driver's seat and learn to steer in a confident, calm, and knowledgeable way, and your life will travel along safely and happily.

HOME FROM PLAY

We must learn the fine art of paying complete attention to life without holding onto it. Children naturally want to play with life. Although we must grow up and take our rightful place in the world as adults, the trick is to regain the lightness of a happy, secure child. The Divine parent not only dreamt us into existence but guides us through life until, after enough play, it gladly takes us back Home.

CHAPTER 22

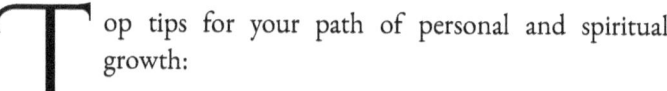

Top tips for your path of personal and spiritual growth:

1. Listen way more than you talk.
2. Learn way more than you teach.
3. Try to reduce your ego a little every day.
4. Make a daily friend of your individual spiritual practices, whatever they may be—meditation, prayer, church, nature, loving people, being on your own, trying to improve your inner self, being in the garden.
5. Be kind to everyone, but be very tough on yourself when it comes to understanding what you're doing and saying.
6. Be grateful.
7. Forgive everyone. Be diligent about forgiving anyone from your past who pops into your mind. Eventually, you'll get to the end of the list!
8. Get a spiritual teacher. The teacher doesn't have to call themselves a teacher. In fact, they can be

anyone who teaches you how to be a more evolved person. Choose your teacher by instinct; it won't necessarily be someone you like (or like all the time). But it will definitely be someone who makes you grow.

CHAPTER 23

spiritual processes

There are specific spiritual processes that we continue to do throughout our lives:

1. **healing** the human dimension
2. **connecting** to the Divine

We need both because if we only did the second one (connecting to the Divine), we would have so much unconscious stuff that we wouldn't get anywhere. We wouldn't even know why we weren't getting somewhere. If we only did the first one (trying to heal the constant mess inside us), we would be lifelong psychology students. That wouldn't work because the problems are endless. Even if we could eliminate all our current problems, we bring a tonne from elsewhere.

Ask for the assistance of spiritual teachers who know the way well so that your process is safe. You can ask teachers who are physically present or energetically present. You can ask anyone who has been a spiritual teacher to you—people you've read about, the great spiritual beings who have graced Earth with their presence, or anyone who comes to your mind and is meaningful to you. Say that you want them to be around you while doing these processes. It ensures your safety.

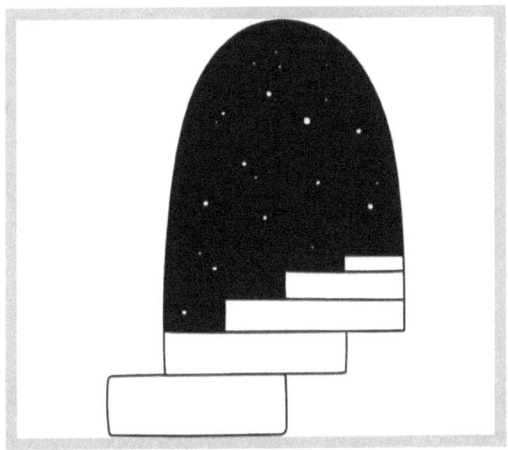

HEALING THE HUMAN DIMENSION

- Whatever wants to come up inside you, sit with it.
- Give it free rein.
- You don't have to decide what to let come up.
- Whatever comes up is the thing that is most pressing for you now.
- You must feel the emotion of it.
- Don't force it.
- Allow it to happen.
- It's burning itself up and letting off steam.
- However uncomfortable anything feels, persevere with it.
- Let it bubble away inside you.
- If it makes you sad, angry, or afraid, go into it.
- If you feel like being angry, then be angry.
- If you feel like crying, then cry.

- Screaming? Then, scream.
- Saying something to someone in your mind, even if it's ridiculous? Then, say it.
- No matter if it is illogical. Emotion is not logical.
- Throw emotion and energy out into the room in any way you can. It helps your body and energy field to release things.
- If nothing much comes up, that's fine, but keep inviting this process because many things will come up with time.

CONNECTING TO THE DIVINE

Try to feel at peace with God and everything. If whatever you're working on hasn't been worked through, it's alright. Sometimes, you won't feel any peace, but keep returning to this step. Sooner or later, when you're not expecting it, you'll notice a sense of peace descending on you. You may have been working on something for a while, but it doesn't seem to be shifting. You may have often asked God for help, but don't feel that help has come your way. Then, one day, you will be walking along, thinking about not much, and you will notice how beautiful everything looks and how unworried you are. God's grace has descended on you.

CHAPTER 24

reality shifting

When you are trying to heal something in yourself, another person, or your environment, you could think of it in two ways:

1. You are changing your current reality (or that of another person) to a healthier, happier version of existence.
2. You are shifting realities to a concurrent but superior version of your current experienced one (for example, on a good day, your world looks and feels very different to a bad day).

Both ways of healing are viable. Both work. Both are indicative of the fact that what we experience as reality is very susceptible to the state of our consciousness.

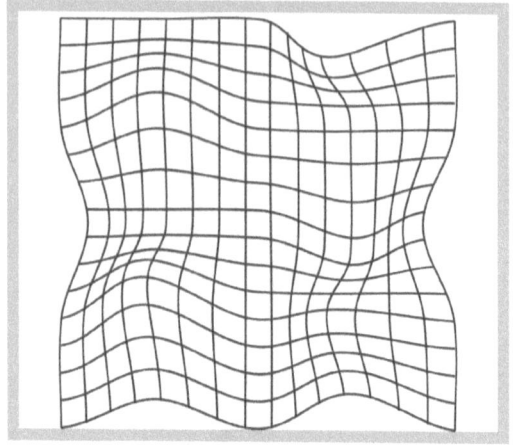

DREAM SHIFTING

Most dreams or visions we create for our lives are bigger versions of what we already know, exaggerations of what we currently perceive. That is okay, but it is not extraordinary. If we want dreams that move us out of our current reality, we must let Life dream up the dreams inside us. That way, they will embrace things not already in our experience, that we do not normally perceive, that we do not yet know we are capable of.

CHAPTER 25

miraculous stats

ZERO TO HERO

My daughter is currently studying statistics as one of her university psychology subjects. It's her least favourite subject, but we joke that, at least, it's not as bad as when I did statistics. The subject was simply beyond me. My maths capabilities were far below what would make the subject understandable. Nevertheless, to pass psychology, I had to pass statistics. I had resigned myself to the fact that I wasn't going to pass and was, most likely, going to get zero.

Then, a most amazing thing happened. My friend, Alex Baturnysky, was very good at statistics. An hour before the exam, my friends and I sat in the university cafe with exam stress glumness. Alex must have seen the rather doomed look on my face. He asked if he could help.

I responded, "Thank you very much, but I am beyond help. Anyway, there is nothing you can do in such a short time."

He persisted and said, "No, let's try."

I really didn't want to try because I was desperately hopeless about it all and frankly hated everything to do with the subject. I listened as best as I could out of politeness. He went through five questions that were the sort of thing that could be asked. He explained in detail what the correct answers would be. Numbers, numbers! For some reason, numbers have always been meaningless to me. Meaningless and entirely forgettable.

You would not believe it, but out of the hundreds of questions that could've been asked in the exam, the five he gave me were the five that were asked. Alex had no inside information. I stood up from the exam and had no idea if the answers I remembered made any sense. I may have written gibberish. Statistics was an incoherent foreign language to me. Maybe I would still get zero.

When the results came out a few weeks later, lo and behold, I got 100% and a high distinction. It was amazing to get the exact five questions, and equally amazing that I remembered the answers. Given my inability to remember numbers, let alone lines of them like a code, the outcome was mind-boggling—more mind-boggling than the statistics.

When Alex found out about my result, he announced to all our friends that I must be a maths genius.

I laughed and said, "No, I'm not a genius."

I tried to explain that I simply repeated what he told me. He would have none of it (I think he had a crush on me at the time) and insisted to our friends that I was, in fact, a genius.

"I know how little she understood the topic," he said proudly. "To go from that to a high distinction from 45 minutes of help—it's unbelievable!"

As Alex would have it no other way, I accepted his prognosis, which seemed to mysteriously disappear when he got annoyed with my lack of interest in him six months later.

CHAPTER 26

no martyrs

When I was fourteen, a missionary visited my school and gave a little talk. Although I can't remember what she said, I remember being impressed with her. I couldn't put it into words, but there was something special about her. It might have been the calm look in her eyes, even though, from what she said, her life was far from calm. She seemed happy without trying to convince anyone that she was.

After the talk, a student I didn't know approached me and said, "I think you are going to be a missionary."

"No," I said. "I don't think so."

It seemed to me that even if one did want to be a missionary, it wasn't the sort of thing that one would admit to. Although the girl didn't appear to have any intention of repeating the conversation, I was well aware that the teenage world can be brutal.

"I saw the look in your eyes when the missionary was talking," said the girl by way of explanation. "I was watching you."

I must have been so absorbed in the missionary's talk that I didn't notice her watching. What the girl said was surprising and thought-provoking, but it wasn't frightening. However, the next thing she said did frighten me.

"I think you will be a martyr," she said in the same matter-of-fact manner.

As we weren't friends, her prediction of my fatal, if not glorious, future didn't seem to bother her in the slightest. She walked off, and for the rest of our schooling days, we never crossed paths again.

Donna as a schoolgirl.

I told myself that the girl knew nothing. However, something in what she said stayed with me. It wouldn't have scared me if I thought there wasn't some truth in it. In my heart, I knew that if it came down to someone else's life and my own, I would probably have to choose the other or I wouldn't be able to live with myself. I was indeed likely material for martyrdom. Of course, I didn't want to be a martyr. Who wants to die? I didn't want to sacrifice my life, happiness, talents, or anything. Who would?

Eventually, I noticed that the thought of martyrdom had disintegrated in my consciousness. From my spiritual studies and life practices, I learned that, contrary to an unconscious belief that God wants us to suffer, the Divine wants us to be happy. The young girl was unconsciously channelling the idea that people who love God make significant sacrifices, see other people's lives as more important than their own, and act accordingly.

Sacrifice is not the way of the higher spiritual teachings. We learn that there is no value in it. There is only value in healing, peace, and seeing life aright. God doesn't want martyrs. The Divine wants the expression of its harmonious, creative, and beautiful being. That sounds happy, right? The only thing we sacrifice is the ego. And that is no sacrifice when we realise how flawed, troublesome, and destructive it is.

No one has to be a martyr. On the contrary, everyone should be entirely selfish. Not selfish in the usual sense of the word, but selfish in the way of knowing that the spiritual path means we value everything that adds to our well-being.

When we love, we live with connectedness.
When we forgive, we feel stress-free.
When we create, we live with inspiration.
When we follow inner direction, we feel alive.
Is that even a choice?

CHAPTER 27

light bearers

HANDS-ON-HEALING

LIGHT BEARERS

I first learned hands-on healing when I was twenty and happily belonged to a Catholic Charismatic Community. It was one of my favourite things to do. I never doubted its authenticity because, to me, it seemed obviously real and beneficial.

I remember attending a community conference in a different state. At that stage, I didn't have any money. I was thrilled to be gifted the conference and flight tickets. The conference was a large, enthusiastic gathering with hundreds of people (predominantly young adults) fired up with spiritual energy.

Attending the spiritual conference with some of my community in 1981. I am front row, far right.

One hands-on-healing session had a particularly long line. I waited patiently for my turn with the prayer healers. They were girls my age—young but sincerely doing their best. As I knelt for them to put their hands on my shoulders, I told myself that it didn't matter whose hands were on me because the power of God was running through them. I raised my arms and turned my palms and head Heavenwards. It was a beautiful moment of light. Afterwards, I thanked the girls and trotted off.

Later, in the bathroom, I overheard one of my friends say to another friend, "Two of the healers asked me who our friend is. I told them her name is Donna and asked why they wanted to know. They said they were surrounded by light when they prayed for her and that there was something special about Donna's calling. Do you think we should tell her?"

They did tell me because they were lovely girls. I thanked my friends and changed the conversation to something else. This experience has always stayed in the back of my mind. I remember the profound feeling of light when I was being prayed for. I also remember that it was very affirming to have strangers acknowledge my calling. In our earthly world, a spiritually oriented person has to put up with a lot of misalignment. It was a welcome change.

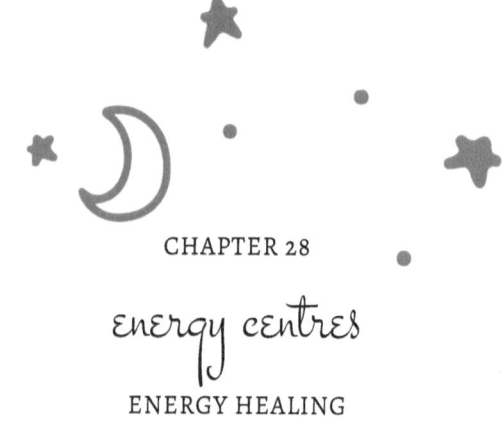

CHAPTER 28

Energy centres
ENERGY HEALING

Charismatics and Pentecostals generally place their hands on the person's shoulders for healing. If we add to that the Eastern knowledge of the seven main chakras, it becomes a small step for the healer to place their hands on the body's various energy centres.

It goes without saying that the healer must have the

capacity to heal, or more precisely, the ability to let the healing channel flow through them. Otherwise, hands-on healing can feel like an invasion of personal boundaries or like nothing at all. In everyday life, I do not generally move into other people's energy fields because it would be intrusive for them and exhausting for me.

Sometimes, when working with a healer, a person can heal instantly. Whatever problem they had can disappear before they walk out the door. In such situations, it is a combination of the person's openness, the previous working through of the problem, the healer's capability to connect with the healing forces, timing, and destiny. People often seek help at the tipping point of a problem when it seems the darkest, but dawn is just over the horizon.

The timing of healing is neither the healer's concern nor the recipient's. We do our best. The rest is up to things beyond our control. If the individual keeps moving in the healing direction, things will change beneficially. The person will grow in ways they hadn't imagined. The intention to get well adds much fuel to progress.

The ability to heal ourselves and others automatically comes to all serious spiritual students once they reach a certain point in their evolution. Ultimately, our soul is in the healing hands of the Divine. They are the majestic invisible Hands that moulded our form and continue to nurture our spirit.

CHAPTER 29

angels from the dust

I come from a family of Australian farmers. My grandfather was a pioneer farmer, and his son and grandson were also farmers.

My grandfather built this home, Little Oakey, in outback Australia. He is with family members on the verandah.

As children, we spent many carefree, unrestrained holidays enjoying farm life. My father died when I was in my last year of school, and my uncle, who was running the family farm, kindly took it upon himself to be our proxy father. He knew my father would have been very proud that I was at university, and he watched with interest to see how my great professional career was going to unfold. He was not impressed to find out that one of my main jobs after graduating from university was teaching religion in schools.

I recall him throwing his arms in the air, storming out of the room in exasperation, and saying, "Religion? Religion! What sort of a job is that? Teaching Hail Marys!"

He felt I was throwing away my good mind, education, and talents. He did the same when I spent much of my time working voluntarily with the homeless people of inner Sydney. He felt someone else could look after them and that I was wasting my life. I never dared to tell him that, at one point, I seriously considered joining a religious order of nuns. Australian rural culture is not an easy match with the spiritual path. Spirituality and the outback are not a natural marriage.

To balance things out, I also recall another story. One day, the elderly mother of that uncle was hanging out clothes on the old wire clothesline held up by branches. She looked up from the vast dusty earth into the even vaster blue sky and saw the image of a face in the clouds. She said she did not know if it was an angel or me, but it made her feel much better. She died not long after that.

love matters

BOOK 2 OF SWEET SPIRIT SERIES

introduction

WHAT REALLY MATTERS

Love Matters begins with the physical dimension, progresses through the interrelational, and moves to the spiritual. If we wish to be at our best, we must address all the levels of our being. Physically, we need to be on track with our output, input, and the subtler task of maintaining the five elements that make up our body. Mentally, we should imbibe what pushes our mind in the direction we wish to travel. Emotionally, we need to connect with people in an honest and life-affirming manner. Spiritually, we must keep centring ourselves through silence, meditation, contact with nature, and everything that recalibrates and elevates our consciousness.

This second book of the *Sweet Spirit Series* is given to you with love and respect for your personal development, health, happiness, and spiritual evolution. It will help you connect more directly and purposefully with your intrinsic spiritual identity. It will lessen loneliness, worry, and ill health and increase connection, peace, and wholeness. It will help you to enlarge your energetic influence, deepen your involvement with life, and expand the scope of your creative spirit. *Love Matters* will help you with what really matters.

INTRODUCTION

Today is a new day,
a good day,
a learning me,
a better me.

I will walk out my door
with the confidence
of someone who walks
with grand companions.

Whatever I was yesterday,
it is gone.
My mind is devotedly
waiting on my instructions.

I will bubble with
a brightness that pulls
the good towards me
and those I love.

I will bounce around the negativity
and come to the end of the day
as a clean, vibrant,
growing creation.

PART ONE

physical matters

BODY AND ITS ENVIRONMENT

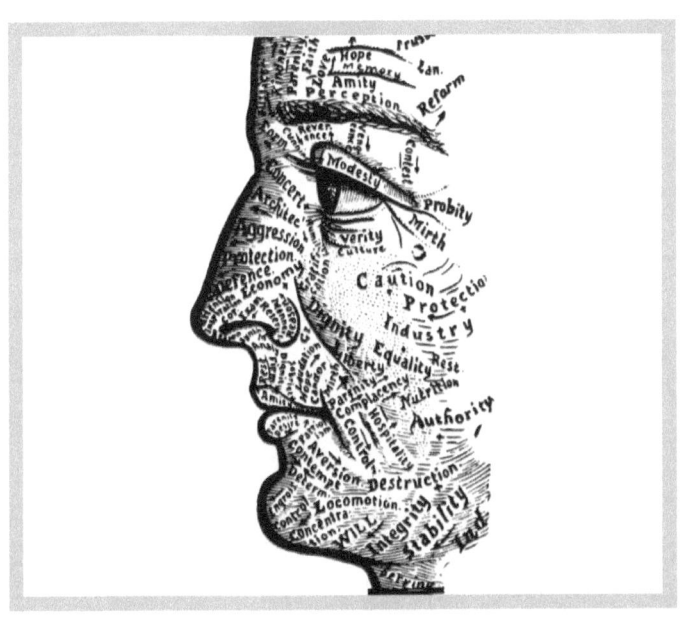

CHAPTER 1

spotlights

BODY

BODY AS FIRST LOVE

FIRST LOVE

If we cannot love our own body—the incredible, dynamic, capable creation God gave us—we will not be able to love the rest of us, let alone the rest of humanity.

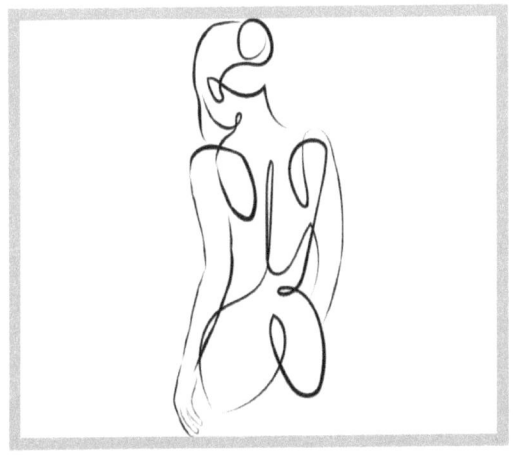

BALANCE

Balance the masculine and feminine in you. It is not about gender but quality of consciousness. Our consciousness must be fully functioning and alive with the best of feminine

wisdom, creativity, intuition, and heart

and the best of masculine

energy, courage, logic, and the drive to make, change, and fix things.

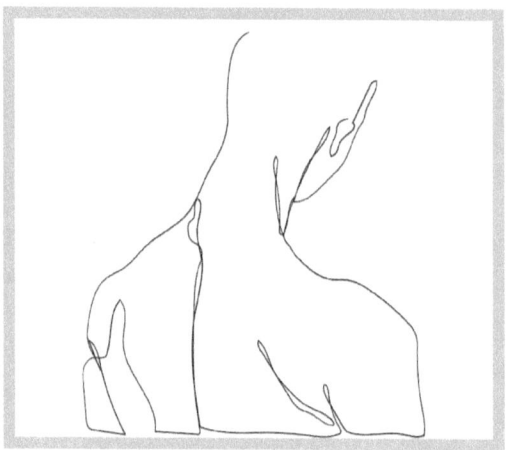

IDENTITY

Don't define yourself by gender, profession, religion, beliefs, orientation towards anything, or any of the countless other identities that emerge from the human experience. These things make a very limited way of seeing yourself. Although you may recognise these aspects as part of your human self, if you want to be happy and fulfil your potential, you must see them as shadows, not foundational structures. Your spiritual identity is your unshakeable, unquestionable, earthquake-proof identity.

DON'T DRAG

When conscious of maintaining our health at the various levels of our being, we naturally think of doing many simple things that make a big difference. For instance, don't use your hands and arms to drag yourself up from a chair. Use your core muscles and legs. Being aware will lead to many bright ideas, and they will be specifically tailored to us.

BOTOX BODY

While there's nothing wrong with looking our best, our *best* is predominantly an inside affair. With modern technology and money, people can make themselves look considerably ageless. However, it is not the right type of agelessness. If we age gracefully and with minimal intervention, then we and those around us are reminded of the movement of time and the preciousness of life. Otherwise, the botoxed face can get quite a shock when death does not heed its camouflaged face.

WEIGHING IT UP

Don't think of your scales as a foe but as a friend. It can help keep you on track with your physical health and well-being. I use mine at the end of most days to monitor what's happening inside my body. Did I overeat? How is my digestive system working? Did today's exercise affect my body mass? You can tell a lot by the small changes in your weight before it develops into major problems.

Everything can be used either positively or negatively. Even the so-called negative things and situations in life can be used to your advantage (at the very least, as a learning tool) so that your entire life is seen as one helpful event leading to the next.

SAFE TRAVELS

Look after your body. You need it to carry you through life without undue suffering. Some physical problems will come your way because that's the nature of life, but many illnesses and ailments are entirely avoidable. Be proactive about the information and ideas you get to help fix the issues. Don't be apathetic, fearful, or lazy. You will travel best with a well-functioning, relatively pain-free body.

IDEAL STATE

When the body is quiet and not complaining, which is its ideal state, we don't need to think about it. It's there to do what we want, and that's all.

UNSTICKING OUR BODY

Although it may seem strange, the body is nowhere near as real and concrete as we think. It is a manifestation of our thoughts, a construct of consciousness (mostly unconscious). Understanding this is a tremendous aid to healing. If we made our body, then it can be made in a different way. Merely considering the possibility that the physical comes from the mental will loosen the stuckness of our bodies.

WHICH WAY?

If you are suffering from ill health, it is important to keep reassuring yourself that you are going to get better. Your body is highly attentive to your thoughts and words, soaking them in like a child. You want your mind and energies to move in the direction you wish to go.

USER'S MANUAL

How offensive to God, who has made countless things perfectly, to think that the Creator has made you faulty or of no real value. God makes only good goods. However, you might need to understand the user's manual to know how you work best.

MOVING

Most bodies tend to be quite lazy. They need encouragement, sometimes ordering, to move. For this reason, we need a proactive approach to moving. No matter our age, we must ask ourselves, "How can I move today? What does my body need?" Even when we have physical problems, we must find ways to keep moving.

REMAKING OURSELVES

In dedicated physical disciplines such as yoga, qigong, martial arts, dancing, and sports, we have to eliminate our body's unconsciousness and laziness. We then deliberately and precisely remake our body how we want it to be. We can apply the same discipline and awareness to our mental and energetic structures.

COURAGE AND VIGOUR

Don't overprotect yourself or your child from the difficulties and challenges of life.

1. From a physical point of view, if we are only used to comfort, our bodies become spoiled and unsuitable for life's rigours. Go out into the weather and don't always be in climate-conditioned environments. Encourage your child to be in touch with the cycles of nature.
2. From a mental point of view, embrace life's challenges and new ideas with courage and vigour. When you fall, get up again. If we protect ourselves too much, we won't be emotionally strong enough for new situations, people, and places.

MOVE IT

If your thoughts or emotions are troubling you, do something with your body. Dance, sing, walk, work out at the gym, play sport, run, swim, climb, or do yoga. The needed attention will drag you away from the rotating whirlwind of your mind or the descending staircase of your emotions.

LIGHTEN UP

Those in the southern hemisphere shouldn't sleep with their head facing south, and those in the northern hemisphere shouldn't sleep with their head facing north. As magnets attract metal, the poles attract the metallic elements inside us. If our head faces the pole, our body's metallic elements will move towards our brain, which is detrimental to our health.

We want to align our body's physical and energetic system with the Earth's magnetic field.

EAT OUTSIDE

Whenever you can, eat outside, preferably in a natural environment. It helps your body to sync with the food you are about to eat and the earth from which both your body and the food are made. Also, never eat unconsciously, mindlessly shovelling in food from who knows where and with no awareness that it is the foundational structure of your human existence. The food you eat graciously becomes the body that gives you the opportunity to live on Earth. It is no little thing. Use it wisely, and it will improve your health and longevity.

MONEY MATTERS

Whenever you are worried about money, reframe it in terms of flow. We have to constantly give to the world in whatever ways we can, including money, work, love, and contributions, and then it will have its own way of coming back to us. Withholding money, work, love, and contributions will stop the flow of money to us.

NO BOUNDS

If you want more money in your life, don't say things like, "I hope I get more money", "I hope I get the job", "I hope this project succeeds". See yourself, your work, and your projects as aligned with the life energy you want. See it as already so. See your existence as positive, successful, abundant, loving, and fulfilling. After all, the reason you want money is to be able to have the life that you want. That life is made from energy, and energy knows no bounds.

SEXUALITY AND INTIMACY

TOUCH

Touch is a conveyor belt for energy. Make sure the energy you're transferring is positive and life-enhancing.

> *Don't harm.*
> *Don't sponge.*
> *Don't freewheel.*
>
> *Be whole.*
> *Be giving.*
> *Be light.*

TOGETHER

There is a strong belief that physical unity brings togetherness. Physical joining is only skin deep. However, when the physical is imbued with the emotional and energetic, it takes on a beautiful, refined, uplifting dimension.

KARMA COLLECTION

The more prolonged and recurrent close physical contact is, the more significant the positive or negative impact will be on those involved. Be careful who you are physically close to. It's not nothing. It holds a lot of power. Those who readily sleep with others take on a lot of karma from different people. They will become mentally fragmented and lose their sense of energetic groundedness. That is why some people on the spiritual path do not get involved in physical relationships. They don't want to collect karma. They have decided to lessen it in this lifetime.

BODY-BASED RELATIONSHIPS

If you approach relationships primarily on the basis of being a body, you will be susceptible to being used and/or rejected. Or if you seem to be winning with sexual conquests, you will have to live with the guilt of hurting people and the restlessness of unsatisfying human connections. There is a better way.

PLEASURE PATH

As we develop, we become less fascinated with the pleasures of the physical dimension. It is not out of denial. When you have something more remarkable, the lesser is no longer esteemed in the same way. The physical, in all its aspects, including the sexual, has its place. And other people's needs must be considered, as well as our own, when we are in a relationship. However, the whole thing is seen differently when one comes into contact with pleasures that make physical pleasure seem pale in comparison. Further, the energetic intimacy that comes from connecting to another in a profound and lasting way supersedes all other forms of intimacy.

A THOUSAND GIFTS

Every day, the power behind the Universe gives us a thousand gifts hoping to catch our eye and win our love: the smiling flower, the laughing child, the loyal partner, the sheltering home, the gracious tree, the warming sun, the calming ocean, the peaceful moon, the energising wind, the healing water, the invigorating music, the inspiring book, and a million other presents from life.

AGEING PROCESS

LITTLE LIGHTS

You should feel that it is a precious time when you are older. Don't entertain the thought of your life *being over*. From a spiritual point of view, it's the opposite. This is your time. You have collected wisdom from life, from working all those years, and all the good and bad things that have happened to you. You will get new ideas, little lights of ideas. Let the ideas grow and the little lights glow. You want your energetic system to become so light and bright that you will wonder why it took you so long. Every morning, when you wake up, feel that now is the best time of your life.

INERTIA

A large part of ageing is that people stop moving. They give in to the considerable downward pull of inertia in their bodies and minds. You don't have to fight life, but you do have to make an effort to be awake and active. Make an effort every day, every year, and every decade of your life, and you will feel that you have genuinely made the most of the precious gift you have been given.

ANVIL OF LIFE

Do not accept that sickness, contagion, and ageing are inevitable. Use your body. Generally, the more you use it, the stronger it will get. If sickness comes your way, treat it as a temporary and uninvited guest who will soon be gone. Tell yourself that your mind and spirit are masters of your body. Your body is a piece of metal that rests on the anvil of life and is shaped by the hammer of thoughts.

FLYING TIME

When you are doing something and time is flying by, and you wonder how a few hours could have passed when it only seems like half an hour, you are in your element and following your true nature. In that state, you don't physically age. If it feels like half an hour has passed when it has really been several hours, then you only aged half an hour. It's a bonus!

NONTERMINAL

If you are called upon to help with the terminal illness of a loved one, the best way is to constantly have in mind the impossibility of a soul being terminal. This will be most beneficial in helping them cross the line with peace, confidence, assurance, and readiness for the next stage of their journey.

CHANGE

People who have had a close family member die when they were young do not tend to take life for granted. My father died unexpectedly when I was 17, and it impacted my future life immensely. I was already deeply spiritual, but experiencing how easily a loved life can be taken away gave me an undeniable impetus to follow my own path.

LOVE MATTERS

Thank you for this day.
Thank you for this opportunity.
What do I want to do with my day?
Am I living the way I truly want?

CHAPTER 2
elemental

OUR ELEMENTAL NATURE

Our bodies are made of the five elements:

1. water
2. earth
3. air or wind
4. fire
5. akash or ether

Think of the elements as ingredients for making life. They can be mixed in various ways to create multitudinous life forms. If we respect the elements and keep them vibrant, our bodies will not complain and will serve us well. Element cleansing and strengthening happen naturally when we are in sync with nature because *we* are nature. If we keep the elements balanced, free-flowing, and vital, our health, at every level, will benefit significantly.

Here are some ways to make element cleansing part of your life. Many people do these instinctively without knowing why. If we understand their purpose and benefit, we can do them more often and more consciously.

1. WATER

Water makes up the majority of our body. As such, it should be respected and taken care of. One aspect is the water we drink. Traditionally, water is stored in copper because copper has natural antibiotic properties. It's an easy way to ensure that our water is pure and good for us. Additionally, before you go to bed, put your hand on the container and say a prayer of appreciation. Water has memory.

If you have a bath in your home, use it to realign yourself.

Lying in warm water will automatically help your physical body to relax and your energetic body to release certain negative aspects. Use bath salts as they reduce inflammation. Don't use synthetically made bubble baths or bath bombs. Lighting candles (not artificially scented ones) is beneficial because it combines the water and fire elements. Adding music, such as chanting from a suitable spiritual source, will also help you. If you don't have a bath, which many people don't nowadays because of smaller house sizes, you can buy a portable one. They're quite cheap as they are essentially an adult version of a toddler's paddling pool.

Of course, if you live near the ocean or a river, you can swim there. The waterways are cold where I live, so I don't swim in them, but some people do. It beneficially includes several elements at once—water, earth, and wind.

2. EARTH

FOOD

Your soul is made of spirit, but your body is made of food. Food is made of *earth*. We are earthenware pots holding heavenly contents.

1. **Earthenware**: Be very conscious of what you eat. Your food's vibrancy and life force contribute greatly to your body's energetic well-being. Notice how you feel after eating certain foods, and you will naturally arrive at the best diet for you.
2. **Freshen Up**: A simple practice that can significantly improve the quality of our food intake is not buying "stale" food. In the West, this is generally considered as out-of-date food. However, that is merely the extreme of stale. Before food gets stale in a molecular sense, it ages in an energetic sense. Try not to buy precooked or partially cooked and packaged food. Make what you can yourself.
3. **Dead Food**: Don't store leftovers in the fridge for too long. Some traditions, such as Ayurveda, say that food should be discarded if it is not consumed within a few hours because its vital energy or prana evaporates when stored in the fridge or freezer. Food older than three days is considered dead food. If our typical diet is full of old or dead food, then the tamas or inertia in the food will be powerless to improve our health and, instead, will contribute to ill health.

4. **Exacerbating the Problem**: To add to the problem, food is often reheated in a microwave for ease and quickness. However, microwaves break the bonds between food molecules, which causes further lifelessness.
5. **Shop Sense**: Be aware of which shops you buy from. Sometimes, old-fashioned shops that make simple food on the spot are best for freshness and lack of processed ingredients (if they are diligent and committed to their service).
6. **Season**: Eat what is in season. It will help your body to balance with its natural surroundings, which it's designed to do. Best of all, grow your own vegetables. The cellular structure of your garden produce will align itself with what your family needs. The next best option is to buy produce grown in your local area. Don't fight Mother Nature. Eat what she gives when she gives it. It's that way for a good reason.

Bring more awareness to what you're eating. It's not that,

"You mustn't eat this, or you mustn't eat that." That sort of approach brings resentment and resistance. But when you eat, ask yourself:

- What am I eating?
- Why am I eating it?
- Is this really what I want to eat?

Eat with awareness, not compulsiveness.

There are many elements to consider regarding our individual food needs, and we do not want the process to become authoritarian, joyless, tedious, or fanatical. With open-mindedness, appreciation, and intelligence, we can become more aware of what we feed ourselves and our families. Willingness to learn and readiness to experiment keep us moving in the right direction.

Listen to other people's food ideas with an open mind. Ask the younger generation why they do things a certain way. Although some practices should be reintroduced from the older generations, there are always new approaches from the upcoming generations that may be most appropriate for the current world for both obvious and subtle reasons.

We all have our inner guide and expert on what is best for us. If you become sensitive to your body's internal voice, it will tell you what and how much to eat and drink. For example, If I need more Vitamin C (such as when a cold is trying to come my way), I often dream of a particular juice made mostly of oranges, which is more delicious than anything I have ever tasted in this world.

Get better at listening to your body. Every body is different. Further, it will alter at various times of your month, year, and life. You must work it out by experience, experimentation, and tuning in to what effect multiple foods have on you. It's well worth the effort as it will lengthen your lifespan, increase your ability to pay attention, and heighten your energy levels. If you try to stick to somebody else's prescription or diet, it most likely won't work. Besides, you'll get very bored. If you work it out yourself with intuition and knowledge, it will never be boring because it's what you want to do.

NATURE

Weekly walk in the ranges

Nature is your best helper, and she's free. When I lived in the city, I walked in the nearby parks several times a day. I also drove about forty-five minutes, once a week, into the ranges and walked in the forest. The towering trees set me up for the week. They breathed life into me and sorted out more problems than I knew about. Once a month, I drove two hours to an idyllic seaside village and let the roaring ocean wind, luscious sand, bouncing river, and gentle pace of the forest-nestled town remove the debris from my life.

Now that I live in a beautiful rural town at the bottom of

a mountain, next to a forest, with a creek running beside my house, my connection with nature is fortuitously unbroken. However, for forty years, I had to organise my city life to have sufficient contact with nature. It wasn't really enough for someone of my disposition, but it was enough to get by.

CLOTHES

Being conscious of what you wear can help you align more closely with the earth element. Your clothes affect your body and energy system. Try to wear natural fibres as much as possible.

Also, look at the reasons behind your choice of clothes. You are free to dress as you desire, but let it be a conscious process. It will change over the years and even over the day. You can dress however you want, but make sure it works for you and not against you. Let your clothes be an extension of your spirit so that they are helping you move in the direction you want.

In my twenties, I went through a stage of loving red. Red is robust and vibrant, which I wasn't at that stage. So, I liked its assistance. These days, I have fire on-call when needed and only have one piece of red clothing. I have always loved sky blue, which is very calming.

Dressing deliberately and with understanding will save you a small fortune when buying clothes. You won't be labelled, which is expensive. And you won't tend to make buying mistakes. When I go clothes shopping, I buy quickly and decisively. I try something on and ask myself, "Is this mine?" Then, I let intuition answer. It's an easy yes or no—decision made in one second.

3. AIR OR WIND

Breathe fresh, clean air as much as your living circumstance allows. If you live in polluted air, go to the country whenever possible. The sort of air you breathe affects you, as does the way you breathe. Get to know your breathing patterns. You are alive because of your breath. Use yoga breathing exercises (pranayama) to help regulate and strengthen your breath. That, in turn, will open energetic doorways for you.

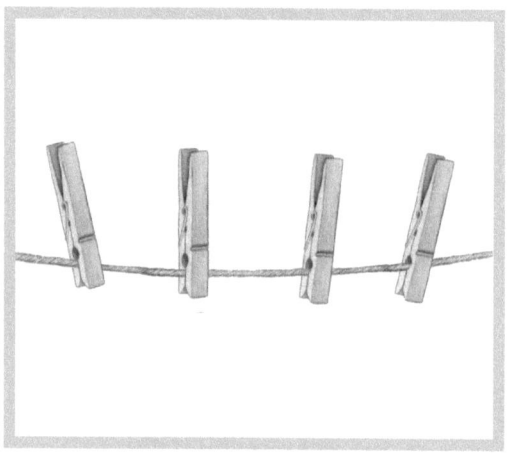

Weather permitting, consider drying your clothes on an outside washing line rather than using an electric clothes dryer. You will save on your energy bill and be working with nature. Let the sun and wind bring their beautiful, impactful energy into your clothes, which will then transfer into you. The long winters where I live are unsuitable for outside drying, but the end of spring heralds the reintroduction of the garden clothesline.

One of the wind-related practices I frequently do is to go for windy drives. As I live rurally, going for beautiful drives close to me is easy. I put all the windows down so the wind rushes through the car and my etheric system. The wind is exceptionally cleansing. Everyone feels better after a windy walk on the beach. Ideally, the wind is at a specific mild temperature. You will automatically relax and feel at one with it. If it's very hot or cold, do your best. I still do my windy drives in winter and dress accordingly.

4. FIRE

Although the fire element is relatively small in our elemental constitution, it is powerful. If there is too much fire, the person will become unbalanced, burn up, and spread destructive energy. Too little, and we cannot light up on the inside. We need fire to create, enjoy our lives, and pulse with enthusiasm.

1. Sunlight is fire, so make sure to get some every day.
2. If you are a camper, you will know a campfire's enticing and bewitching impact.
3. Wood-burning fires in homes, whether open hearths, enclosed fireplaces, or stoves, not only add to the atmosphere of the home but also cleanse the aura.
4. Oil-burning lamps and candles (not artificially scented) also connect us to the fire element.
5. In the East, there are traditional fire cleansing practices called Klesha Nashana Kriya, which means to burn up impurities. I participated in one

at the Isha Yoga Centre in Melbourne and loved it. It was in a small, darkened room with a sacred feeling. Containers with fire and bunches of neem leaves were moved in patterns around the participants. The meridian lines are followed in a particular order so that the akashic body surrounding the physical body becomes free of gathered impurities.

5. AKASH OR ETHER

Akash or ether is expansion, the space between the space. It is the energetic environment of the other four elements. Just as water has memory, akash has intelligence. Some people unknowingly connect with this spacious dimension and are blessed accordingly. Others constantly work against the akashic order and suffer as a result. We aim to become more aware of the etheric dimension and tap into the akashic storehouse of knowledge, which is like a vast, invisible library or internet. That is how some people seem to spontaneously know things, sometimes without knowing where they come from.

Meditation is the most direct route to the akashic order. Another way is to become available to the energy of sunrise and sunset. Try to time your waking so that you can see the sunrise. You don't have to be outside, but it's better if you are. At least, go outside for a minute or two and breathe in the delightful, energised atmosphere of the breaking morning.

The time before and after sunrise and sunset are ideal for

spiritual practices. There is a cradling point in nature between day and night. It is as if nature is holding its breath as it transforms into something else. If we are still, we are helping that process to also happen in our physical and energetic bodies.

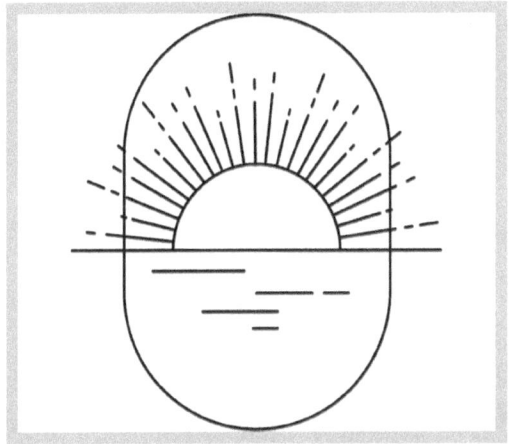

This can beneficially affect our health, peace of mind, and spiritual groundedness. Many people do this naturally. They instinctively want to sit with the sunrise and watch the sunset. Nature wants to help you. You have two opportunities to connect with the sun's rising and setting every day. They are among the most energetically useful and powerful aspects of material existence.

CHAPTER 3

body and spiritual practices

SIT DOWN

There are many reasons why it's good to sit on the floor for spiritual practices. It makes us more grounded and gives us a better base from which to work. Our energy systems are intrinsically connected with our bodies, and getting our bodies properly aligned is primary. Some spiritual practices are not for sitting, such as walking in nature, but many are. With practice, you will see that they work better on the floor, not in a chair.

It can take Westerners quite a while to make sitting on the floor comfortable and correct, but if we don't try, then it certainly won't happen. It requires a strong spine and open hips, which most Westerners do not have, all the more so if you're not young. Some people are flexible without effort, but it generally requires work and attention. No one is strong without effort.

A cushion is very useful in the early stages. You don't need to spend money on proper yoga cushions. You can make your own from a folded blanket or towel. It must be dense, not soft like a lounge cushion or bed pillow. Gradually reduce the height of your cushion. A couple of minutes of simple hip-opening exercises whenever you think of it (particularly before you sit on the floor) will help. It only takes a few years of sitting on the floor with moderate effort to make a huge difference to your hips and reach the point of a relatively correct and comfortable posture.

A chair is fine if you can't or don't want to sit on the floor. The most important thing is to do the practice. However, don't lounge back in the chair. Keep as straight as you can without too much strain. And don't lean your head on anything. Your neck needs to be free and relaxed because of energy flow. You can imagine sitting cross-legged on the floor while in the chair, trying to have the same straight-backed posture.

EMPTY STOMACH, FULL PRACTICE

The more intense spiritual practices are always done on an empty stomach. Food takes 40 minutes to 2 hours to be processed and moved out of your stomach into your small intestines. For spiritual practices, it generally doesn't matter if the partly processed food is in your intestines. It only matters if it's still in your stomach. The more food is there, the more problematic it can be. After a meal, much of the body's focus is on digestion. That is not conducive to meditation and breathing practices. Doing some higher-level yogic practices with a full stomach could make you sick.

Sometimes, an empty stomach is not possible because of work and family commitments. In that case, eat lightly and finish the rest later. Avoid meat as it digests slowly. Also, avoid a big hit of carbs. Fruit and vegetables are processed quickly, so they are ideal. Keep away from caffeine before your practice, and obviously, stay away from addictive substances such as alcohol, marijuana, and nicotine. None of this should be compulsive or fanatical. It is a matter of looking at it clearly, experimenting with what works best, and moving in that direction.

MOVE FIRST, SIT SECOND

Before we do stationary spiritual practices, it is best to do a physical practice or to have done one earlier in the day. If our body is restless and disconnected, so will be our invisible bodies. Everything about us is connected. When we do a spiritual practice, it's good to start from the bottom—our body. The point is not physical prowess, although that can be a good goal in itself. The holistic point of the movement is that it helps us align our energy systems into a calm, receptive state.

SUN AND MOON PRACTICES

Without the sun, we would be nothing. The sun is the basis of every life form in our world. Imagine that you're gathering the sun's energy to give you the fire you need to be healthy and activated. Know that the sun is graciously and happily sharing itself with you. The sun is a masculine energy. Its heat, vitality, and power have an enormous ability to create and also destroy.

The moon is feminine, soft, and subtle. It is water-based, which is feminine. The moon is responsible for the rise and fall of the tides and all other water forms, including the water in us. We are predominantly water. The full moon brings out, exacerbates or exaggerates whatever state you are in. Mentally unwell people tend to feel more unwell when it is full moon, thus the saying *lunatics*. Happy and peaceful people tend to feel more so on full moon. Meditative people become more highly meditative. Go outside on full moon and feel the different energy in the atmosphere. Even the trees seem to lean towards its mystifying glow. Everything responds to the light of the moon. Take it into your being and use it to heighten your intentions for life.

CHAPTER 4

home

The energy in your home greatly affects you and your family. It's not neutral. It has a real impact, for good and bad. Make it add to your well-being. When you move into a new house, use the elements to clean it and make the energy field vibrant and positive.

Water is your best friend when it comes to cleaning. However, there are also other subtler ways to clean:

- **Fire** is a powerful cleansing agent. You can use natural candles, organic oils in oil burners, smudging sticks, and pure incense sticks. Anything made locally is a bonus as it will be in sync with your nearby surroundings (particularly if all its ingredients are also locally produced).
- If you live rurally or in treed suburbs, open windows to access fresh, clean **air**. Apartments in polluted cities don't have this option.
- Use chanting, recorded meditations, or spiritually energised music to fill the air with harmonic **sound**.
- All our objects are made from the constituents of **earth**. Those constituents transform according to our use and handling of the objects. Don't let rubbish accumulate as it has a distasteful energy. Don't allow unnecessary and excessive objects to be stored in your cupboards, as they also carry a specific type of energy that works against your balance and freedom. Clean-ups are important not only from an aesthetic sense but also from a very real and impactful energetic sense. You will never delete unwanted karma from your life if you cannot even delete the gross physical counterparts of it.
- Your home acquires your energy simply by you living in it. So, if your house needs an energy update, the most effective solution is to update your own energy through awareness and **spiritual practices**.

CHAPTER 5
face value

If you show me a photo of someone, I will, more often than not, have instant access to a great deal of information about them. Not personal details, but an understanding of where their soul is and the types of problems they will tend to have. It doesn't always work because some photos are set up professionally to look a certain way, which disguises much of the information. Also, some people have learned to hide their energy behind a facade and become somewhat impenetrable, but they are few and far between. Most people cannot help but be themselves.

Along the way with buying and selling houses, I have discovered that the same thing applies to house photos. Houses, for me, are all about energy—the energy of the current house, its history, the people who lived in it, and the vibration of the garden (which comes from the person who has tended to it).

About ten years ago, I was downscaling from a large suburban home to a small inner-city house. The gentrified suburb I had my eye on was in high demand. I found an original cottage that needed repair and was reasonably priced. It had been owned by several generations of one family. The first in the family to own it was one of the lucky young soldiers who returned from Gallipoli in 1915. He was able to buy the house for a few thousand pounds. It was then passed on to his son and family, who lived there for sixty more years.

The house felt right. It's not that it had a perfect energy—far from it. Of the children belonging to the last owners, one died in an accident as a young adult, and not long after, another became paraplegic from a botched surgery. The house knew tragedy. Nevertheless, it had the balanced energy of a small space that had housed and fed lives, loves, loss, and the everyday routines of talking, crying, arguing, laughing, eating, cleaning, washing, and sleeping.

Although I felt it now belonged to me, it appeared it would be sold to someone else. Standing outside the little house, I asked the real estate agent if something similar was available.

"Of course," he replied enthusiastically in typical real estate fashion. "Let me show you some of them."

He opened his folder and started to tell me about the first house. As I could instantly tell that the house wasn't right and he looked like he was going to spend five minutes on each house, I interrupted.

"No," I said decisively.

He looked surprised but turned the page.

"No," I said before he got one word out.

He began turning pages, one after the other, as I took a momentary glance and said, "Next."

After about twenty houses, he laughed and closed the book.

There was no use trying to explain anything. He stood there awhile and said, "Let me get back to you about this house."

I got the house.

CHAPTER 6

don't give your sleep away

We must outgrow the tendency to look at sleep as a reprieve from the day's problems, a welcome lapse into unconsciousness. Our body needs the physical rest of sleep, but our consciousness does not. It never sleeps. It works all through the night on something or other. That "something" will determine how we wake up and many other things as well. If you go to sleep unconsciously, it will be the perfect breeding ground for everything negative to percolate, manifest, and grow. The state in which you enter sleep will be magnified during the night.

1. Without increasing them, gently become aware of your worries, fears, angers, and sorrows before you sleep. You may not be able to get rid of them, but the mere act of becoming objectively aware of their presence already lessens their potency.
2. Listen to a settling meditation or do your own meditation practice before you drift into slumber. Don't pick an energising meditation or one that activates the lower three chakras—root, sacral or

solar plexus. Choose a meditation that resonates with your heart, throat, third eye or crown chakra. Additionally, be careful whose voice you are listening to. Energy transfer through voice can be very powerful, inviting that person into the sanctuary of your inner self.

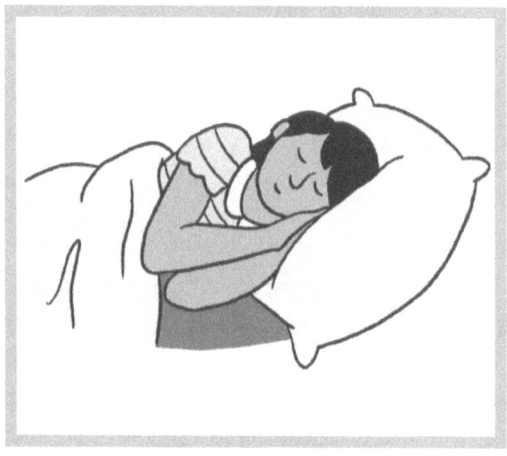

CHAPTER 7

Wheeling and Dealing

My car was in a crash, and I had to replace it. My financial advisor (oldest son) told me it wasn't a good time to upgrade. To make it easy, I should buy the same make and model. I know little about cars and took my youngest son with me, who was about twenty then. He didn't know a lot more than me.

I looked at the prospective car briefly and then at the seller more closely. Satisfied with both, I offered him $12,000, which was $1,000 less than the advertised price.

"Look," he said, "I can't accept anything less than..."

Oh dear, I thought. *I will have to offer closer to the asking price of $13,000.*

"$11,000," he said adamantly.

"$11,000?" I asked, wondering if I had misheard.

"Yes," he replied. "It was my sister-in-law's car. She hardly ever used it, which is why the mileage is so low. She died this year, and...well, it's time to sell it."

We shook hands, and that was that. Clearly, we had our own way of doing business.

When the man had gone back inside, my son shook his head and said, "That was weird!"

CHAPTER 8
frictionless fields

The faster and more effortlessly we want something to move, the less friction it should have.

1. The less friction in the **body,** the better it works. The more friction, the more clunky it will be. With little friction in the body, we tend not to feel

it. It won't feel sick. Nor will it feel well. It will be moving along quietly. That's our goal.
2. Our **relationships** also become clunky with friction and irritations. Sometimes, arguments are necessary, and sometimes, arguments bring spice. But it's important not to collect karmic debris from upsetting events. When relationships are frictionless, it doesn't mean that they are dull and boring. The intensity and brightness can come out in many compelling ways.
3. The less friction in the energetic or **spiritual** domain of our being, the more access we will have to the higher dimensions. We become increasingly open to the infinite ideas buzzing around us, more connected to the flow of spiritual brilliance, and more aligned with the endless joy and beauty beneath this physical existence. Source becomes the energy stream we live off.

FIELDS OF ELIXIR

According to Chinese spiritual tradition, our three centres are the lower, middle, and upper dantians. Dantian translates as *field of elixir*. We want the special elixir of life in us. It will prolong our existence and give us health and happiness. The dantians are the seats of life energy in humans. The lower one is for vitality (body). The middle one is for love (relationships). The upper one is for wisdom (spirit).

1. **Lower Dantian:** Your lower dantian is just below your belly button. A strong, stable lower dantian is vital for your health and ability to function well in the world. It's where martial artists get their strength from. It's our physical and energetic maintenance centre.
2. **Middle Dantian:** Your middle dantian or energy centre is in your chest. It houses your heart. See it as pulsating and growing bigger. It will connect you to people and life in a warm, heartfelt way.
3. **Upper Dantian:** Your upper dantian is the home of your third eye. It is the centre of intuition and spiritual connection. Openness to your spiritual centre will bring you healing, brightness, and peace.

CHAPTER 9

living and dying

DOT ON THE COSMOS

Birth and death happen to everyone. The births and deaths around us seem hugely important. Our own birth and death seem most important of all. Every single person who ever came here, who is alive now, and who will come here in the future experiences birth and death. That's a mighty lot of people. Everyone pops out of the earth. Everyone goes back to the earth. It's a matter of timing. In such a long expanse of time, human life is extremely short. We existed as an energy centre for a long time before we came here. We will exist for a long time after. In terms of the soul's longevity, a little lifetime is barely a dot on the cosmos. However, while we are here, we must make the most of our time and the abilities we have brought with us. It's the fragile nature of life that makes being here so valuable. We have to live every day as a tremendous opportunity. Then, we will have the courage to make this life precisely how we want it to be.

A GOOD WAY TO DIE

When a soul leaves a body gracefully, it knowingly or unknowingly lowers its life intensity enough to exit the physical body with minimal drama. Elderly folk who manage to pass on peacefully go through a process of gradually and progressively diminishing their life energy. They come and go, exiting and returning until they finally don't return. It is common to see old people sitting in their chairs, barely there, and then they spring back to life until, one day, the back and forth is done. This is an excellent way to die. It carries the least amount of karmic refuse and allows the individual to move forward with less drag.

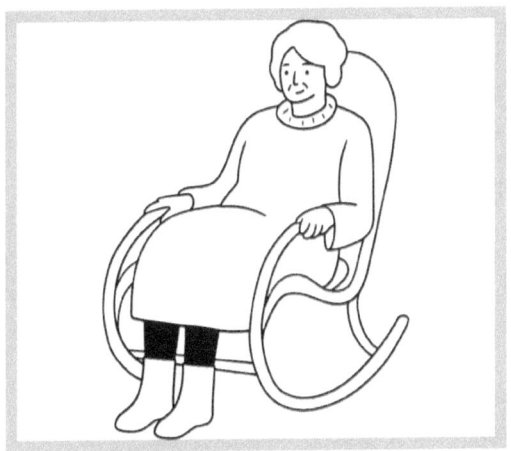

MAHASAMADHI

Occasionally, accomplished spiritual seekers with healthy and robust bodies consciously leave their physical structure by lowering their life force so significantly that they slip out of their bodies. As a result, their body dies. Their soul joins with the infinite ocean of creative power. This process is called *mahasamadhi*.

GENTLY AND GRACIOUSLY

At the end of our lives, we want to go gently and graciously, the same way we gently wafted into our mother's womb—fussless and dramaless. We don't want to be thrown out of the body. We want to leave softly, quietly, and with calm dignity—like a breeze. When a life is thrown from its body suddenly (by accident), semi-suddenly (by an untimely illness), or unwillingly (by resisting death), there is damage to the system because the life force was not prepared to leave. The exiting soul will struggle to understand where it is and what it is supposed to do next. It is a great gift to help someone cross over with grace. The person leaving will benefit from a clearer and calmer post-Earth path.

POST-EARTH

When people die, they essentially follow their instincts and leanings. They are pulled, pushed, and drawn by their inherent tendencies. Advanced souls have a more conscious and intentional path after their passing.

CHAPTER 10

sweet destroyer: Saleha and Mirko

STORY

Mirko and Saleha were seventeen and each other's first love. On the cusp of youth and adulthood, they had a foot in both worlds. They fell in love with each other's beings and then with each other's bodies. Perhaps it happened at the same time. Saleha was a religious girl and had an ongoing battle with her ethics. Her usual response to Mirko's sexual advances was *no*. But Mirko was a young man. His body pushed for physicality. Besides, he was in love with Saleha. His persistence tended to win, one way or another.

They adored each other as young love does. They also fought. Young love has a million misperceptions about life. After all, it wasn't long ago that *boys had boy germs*, and *girls were useless creatures*. The two worlds converge, and there is much to discover.

Mirko said that Saleha taught him to talk. Like many men, their female partners open the world of emotional connection to them and demand that they participate. In return, Mirko showed Saleha the power women have over their men. To be loved as a pure thing is to feel the privilege of responsibility for another's happiness.

Saleha only knew one male body—Mirko's. Other male bodies were disinteresting and somewhat alienating. Mirko's body was interesting and belonged to her. A woman can love her man and not want his body. However, having both adds weight to any relationship. If one thing is not working, the other may be. Between the two, many rivers can be crossed without falling into the water and drifting hopelessly apart.

Long-lasting sex appeal comes from inside us, not from outside. It moves outwards from our inner being. Self-possessed, present, protective men radiate a strong attractor field. Self-possessed, present, caring women also radiate a strong attractor field. All good qualities should be worked on in both men and women, but we must also be our mate's counterpart.

As much as Mirko loved Saleha, he had an eye for bodies other than his mate. He was a good-looking boy with a lot of sex appeal, and it was all too easy to give in to readily available opportunities. Sex appeal and young manhood is a difficult combination to master. Mirko didn't try to master it. He didn't try at all. He went with the flow, believing Saleha would not be hurt because she would never know. The gift of attractiveness must be used cautiously, or its owner will become its slave. It is a sweet destroyer.

For the duration of their relatively long, youthful relationship, Saleha knew nothing about Mirko's wanderings. Only Mirko carried that, and he reaped the karma of shame. Eventually, Saleha outgrew the relationship. It was a painful decision after the innocence and intensity of young love.

Mirko could barely drag himself out of bed in the mornings after their split. He was grief-stricken. His parents were worried about him. All sensible parents watch their offspring closely after relationship break-ups. The feeling of utter despair can seem like it will never heal at that age. Mirko's mother coerced him out of bed in the mornings and sent him off to work. She blamed Saleha. Mirko was her oldest son. She was never going to like the girl who broke the mother-son spell. A boy needs a mother, but a man needs a lover.

Mirko's father watched him from a respectable distance. He told him, "Don't worry, son. It will pass. I promise you, it will pass. I promise that you will feel better." It was sensible, loving advice for a first-time, love-lost victim of life's dramas. First love is deep, and its demise even deeper.

PART TWO

people matters

WHOLE HOLY RELATIONSHIPS

CHAPTER 11

spotlights
RELATIONSHIPS

CONNECTION AND COMMUNICATION

GIFT OF THE MOMENT

Be open to whoever God sends your way regardless of age, gender, background, likes, dislikes, attractions, and aversions. Treat everyone as a gift of the moment.

COMPULSIVE TALK

People generally think that the best way to connect with others is through conversation. Most conversations involve endless blabbing, which is an outlet for restless minds. Such conversations are neither helpful to the participants nor a way of producing real connection. To speak in a truly connective way, you have to know how to be silent with utter steadiness and lack of compulsion.

SUBSTANTIAL SILENCE

It is a substantial offering to any relationship to be capable of silence—a calm, stable silence that has no nervousness and no desire to be anything.

COMPARATIVE CALLOUSNESS

Most people have such a low capacity to feel joy and contentment that a large proportion of their "happiness" comes from comparing themselves to others and coming out better. A lot of conversations are comprised of discussing other people in the context of comparison. Satisfaction is sought by feeling that one's life is better than another's. When we know that we have everything we could possibly need within ourselves, it becomes nonsensical to compare to another person.

SEEDS OF INSECURITY

Judging everything and everyone is so deeply embedded in our consciousness that we have no idea we are doing it. Judging is an ego device for making us feel better. However, judging and comparative thinking plant seeds of insecurity and misery.

IRREPLACEABLE

Egoic love sees people as replaceable and relationships as competitive in value. Spiritual love sees everyone as unique and relationships as being equally so.

SEEN AND LOVED

The heart seeks to be clearly seen, unselfishly loved, and given the freedom to live as it wishes. If you conduct all your relationships in this way, fear will not have a place, and everything around you will tend to grow happily.

FLIRTING

Some people become master flirters. Flirting can boost other people's self-esteem and lift their day. However, its limitations should be clear. The flirt can pay a high price if they play with people's feelings. The karma in such situations often means that the person is not blessed with a substantial and happy relationship themselves. So, if you want to flirt, do it for positive reasons only and make sure, to the best of your ability, that your flirting does not hurt anyone.

A PLACE TO EXPRESS

Make all your interactions and relationships a place to express your God-being. Make them a place to shine the qualities from the Source that pass through your being into the world.

ALONE NOT LONELY

People who are aligned with their spiritual nature enjoy being alone. However, out of a sense of love, compassion, and purpose, most spiritual people make it their business to interact with others.

COUPLE LOVE

ADD VALUE

If you want to become important to someone, make yourself valuable to them. Add value to their life, not in the way you necessarily want, but in the way they want. Care about their needs and what makes them happy. You will naturally become valued by that person.

MAKE IT WORK

If you want your relationships to work:

1. give more than you take
2. have a poor memory
3. don't expect people to work outside the limitations of their current understanding of life

COUPLING

In the human experience, enormous importance is put on couple relationships. Your loved one is precious, and it's vital to love them deeply. However, as spiritual students, no couple relationship can replace the Divine and our commitment to the spiritual path. Another person can't save us. Another person can't make us happy. Another person can't do any of the things that we are striving for on the spiritual path. We sincerely appreciate the people God has given us and have a profound responsibility towards them. However, we do not put another person or a specific type of relationship in the crucial spot we reserve for our relationship with the Divine. When this is kept sacrosanct, everything else will have a way of working out.

TIME

We only have so much time and energy in this lifetime. We have to decide where to put it. No one can decide this for us or force it upon us. We must choose with our deepest, intuitive self.

FOG

When you feel the love between yourself and another person has evaporated, tell yourself it is still there. It doesn't disintegrate but gets covered with the fog of misunderstanding, fear, and everyday problems.

FIXED AND FIXATED

Relationships fixated on the individuals involved are bound to struggle. If you are both looking forward to a shared goal, such as family, a cause, or the well-being of each other, then the relationship can go on endlessly and relatively harmoniously. Constantly looking at each other will create distrust, fear, and a feeling of entrapment. Looking outwards helps make the relationship a place of trust, security, and a home base from which to go into the world.

NEEDS

People have many different needs, and they change as life progresses. Very few people are so settled and balanced within themselves that they do not need other people. Being honest about why we have relationships and what we get out of them takes away a multitude of problems. Relationships are not some airy-fairy, made-in-Heaven, God-only-knows-how-they-work sort of thing. They are based on needs, met and not.

Acknowledging this and being grateful when needs are met or partially met can transform complaining, begrudging people into grateful, independent people with calm, graceful relationships.

CHANGE FOR THE BETTER

Don't try and force people to change. Help them listen more to their inner self, and they will naturally change for the better.

MISCONCEPTION

Most people see the couple relationship as the ultimate source of happiness. Yet, the reality is generally full of problems. Lasting happiness comes from within by reaching a certain state of consciousness.

FREEDOM

It's vital to keep our freedom. Don't give it away to partner, parents, boss, peer group, or anyone else. We're all different. We're the only ones who know what we are meant to do with this lifetime. It's crucial to live your own life. Don't give that privilege away.

WEED-FREE AND THRIVING

If you want your garden to thrive and be weed-free, you have to work on it. If you want your relationship to be relatively harmonious and capable of withstanding problems, you have to pay attention to it. Neglect and carelessness breed breakdown. Although life, relationships, and individuals are naturally messy, the simple quality of care has saved many a garden and relationship.

PEOPLE PROBLEMS

USE IT

Emotion is a powerful tool. We don't want to get rid of it. We want to use it. Most people find that their emotions rule them rather than the other way around. You can learn to direct your emotions into forming life how you want. In this way, even the "bad" emotions can be used to your advantage, not against you. For example, anger can give some people enough momentum to fix situations that need fixing.

MY MIND

As spiritual students, we have to take responsibility for our own mind. No matter what happens with other people, our first responsibility is fixing ourselves and elevating our own consciousness. That immediately changes the focus. My mind is my choice. Our ability to be at peace cannot be taken away. Once we get in a better state of mind, other people often magically fix themselves too. We are energetically connected.

UP AND DOWN

While the spiritual aspect of our being sits serenely in perfection, our material life does not. Everything in the material world, including our relationships, is up and down—sometimes good, sometimes not, sometimes calm, sometimes worrying. When we understand the nature of the material world and all our arrangements, we are much more forgiving of their limitations.

WHO IS THE GARDENER?

It will make a big difference to your peace of mind to accept that you cannot change the people around you, including your loved ones. You can be clear about ideas that would help, but that's all. Everyone is the master gardener of their own blossoming.

MIND THE GAP

Emotions are a fundamental avenue for us to connect with life. We don't want to get rid of them. However, as we progress spiritually, instead of becoming our emotions, we develop a space between our emotions and our inner being. This space reduces and often eliminates the suffering that accompanies painful emotions.

CONTEXT

We must learn to recontextualise the faults and frailties of others. If hurts and offences are taken personally, there will be an ever-increasing accumulation of bitterness. Many things must be overlooked and unwitnessed. Of course, there is a time for speaking up, but it is generally best to focus on the good, not the bad. It is only in the personal that the capacity for offence arises.

NEITHER GOOD NOR BAD

We, as humans, are so very complex. Rare is one who is completely bad or completely good. We are a mixture. And at different times, we do better than at other times. There is no escaping every wrong deed and even every wrong thought. Life and karma take care of that. All must be correctly and honestly accounted for. Yet, in the midst of it all, we must not demonise people. We must see the good that is there because it will carry the soul onward. Just as the bad must be repaid to God, the good will also stand.

BECOMING

People are not one static thing—all good or all bad. They're a complex mixture of many qualities. Their consciousness changes from day to day and even from moment to moment. We are a becoming entity.

EXTENDED FAMILY

It helps to think of people who are unpleasant towards you as part of an extended family. You can't get rid of them, nor would you want to because you care about them. Sometimes, kindness and extra attention are enough to turn them around. They will no longer see you as an enemy or competition but as someone kind to them. Sometimes, that won't work. In that case, ignore their negative energy and continue your positive life.

PEOPLE POISON

Don't let other people's poison settle in you. Resentments are pools of poison in our own being. We have to take people as they are right now. If they're poisonous at this moment, we move away. If they are not, we hold a clean slate for them to write on. If they start writing ugly stuff, we delete it and go our way. We let the river of life keep us in its healing flow.

SOUL STABILITY

If we keep returning to our still, peaceful inner core, what we hope to build in our lives will flourish. If we are divided within ourselves, we will work against our dearest wishes. Also, other people's intent, which may not be good, can greatly affect us. For our own sake and the sake of others, we need to retain and strengthen our soul's stable home.

WEAK LINK

Although we may have to pay the price for someone else's strong ego, a weak one is worse. A fragile ego is highly vulnerable to intimidation, flattery, and seduction. If we are close to a weak person, they can open the gate for damaging entities to come into our life. If an enemy finds it difficult to attack us, the next place they will go is any weakness in our loved one or close friend.

CONFLICT

When you are entangled in a conflict with no obvious solution, it helps to remember that everything can work out well for everyone involved. No one has to lose. It can be handed over to the Divine, allowing inspired solutions to materialise as if from thin air.

WORRY

Whenever you feel worried about a situation for yourself or those around you and can't seem to fix it, give it to the Divine. Tell yourself that you are loved, and those important to you are also loved. The safest place for everyone is in the heart of the Divine, where things tend to get spontaneously sorted. The most wonderful contribution you can make to anyone's life is being well, stable, caring, and happy yourself.

CHANGING PEOPLE

Don't waste energy trying to change people against their will. We let everyone be themselves, stupid as that often is. When they are ready, they'll come. They'll ask a genuine question. They'll listen to the reply.

DIFFERENT REALITIES

People have different experiences of life and, thus, different beliefs about what reality is. Instead of dismissing other people's realities and truths, know there are other experiences of life and thus different perspectives.

WORK STRESS

Many people feel that the bulk of their unhappiness comes from work stress and the very nature of having to work to support themselves and their families. It is often not until the person retires that they realise they are just as unhappy, albeit from different causes. It is far better to realise earlier in life that most people's stress and unhappiness do not come from their outer situations but from their inner ones. Once we know this, there is room for marvellous possibilities. The outer world can only be changed to an extent, but the inner world can be changed completely. Every little realisation helps us to acquire, maintain, and develop stability and equanimity. Moving from endless suffering to a stable, engaging, and balanced life is an achievable goal.

GOOD VIBRATIONS

If you want something to succeed, you have to get into the vibration of success. That vibration consists of positivity, goodwill, energy, expectancy, intelligence, and gratitude. Know that there are many ways to achieve what you want, not just the one that may be in your mind. Every time you move out of the success frequency, remind yourself to get back into it because the frequency you inhabit most frequently is the one working for you.

AMBITION TO SHARING

If your work or project is not going as well as you want, change your focus. Instead of focusing on a particular ambition that signifies success to you, focus on sharing. You started your venture because of your skills and leanings. Try to orient your direction towards sharing them for everyone's benefit. It will bring a distinct quality of honesty to what you do. You still may not get what you want, but you won't be stressed, and everything will work well one way or another.

FROM WHENCE THEY CAME

We are the sole guardian of our heart. We are the only person who decides which words are allowed in and which are sent back from whence they came. Hurtful words hurt the person who says them. They don't have to get a foot in the door of our inner world unless we want them there.

REFORM MEMORY

Reformulate the memory of your past relationships in terms of the positive, not the negative. It is easy for the egoic mind to remember the negatives of any relationship. However, doing so dishonours another person and imprints bad karma in your system. Do not allow your mind to wander along a downward-pulling track. If you look, there will be many positives in most relationships. Don't let your mind and heart be burdened by worrying and fearful thoughts. Remember the good.

RICHER FOR IT

Everyone who comes into your life enriches it in some way. It may be that they bring qualities that you value and appreciate. It may be that they bring lessons that help you grow and mature.

GRIEF

BLESSED BEING

When we are suffering the loss of a loved one, we don't fight it. The grieving process is accepted for what it is. But when it is time, we let it go because there is ultimately nothing to be sad about. We and our loved ones are no less of a being in the Great Beyond. Without a body, without a personality, without thought, we are no less of a blessed being.

NOT LOST

You have not "lost" your loved ones when they pass on. They and God know exactly where they are. You may not know how to see them anymore, but that does not lessen their existence. When you think of them, instead of it igniting a sense of grief, feel that they are trying to talk to you. This will help you become more familiar with the energetic world, and you will never again not know where someone is.

THINKING OF YOU

Whenever you think of your loved ones who have passed over, know they are thinking of you. Although you cannot see them physically anymore, it is easy to "see" them energetically. They haven't gone anywhere. They're right with you, still loving you. It's just that they're living somewhere that takes a different sort of sight. There is no need for sadness. The Divine wants you to feel happy about the love you had with your passed-over ones and will always have.

STILL STANDING

Everything you loved about someone who has passed is still standing right beside you.

PERFUME OF THE ROSES

One of my spiritual teachers saw a lady in his London office whose daughter had been murdered ten years prior. The woman visited her daughter's grave constantly and couldn't come to terms with the loss. After a while, the healer pointed to the homegrown roses on his desk and said, "They send out their beautiful perfume no matter the weather outside." The idea of the roses being their glorious, God-given selves, regardless of anything happening around them, woke the lady up. Her grief was instantaneously and permanently healed. She took the roses home, and when their time came to wither, she knew that the love of God and her daughter's safety could never succumb to the withering of material existence.

CHAPTER 12

forgiveness

Forgiveness is not the highest of our spiritual goals because when we see life from an elevated point of view, there isn't anything to forgive. There is an overriding sense of peace, love, and wholeness. We see life differently from that perspective. However, getting there is a process. It generally doesn't happen overnight. There are lots of small spiritual steps along the way. Forgiveness is a repeated one.

The practice of forgiveness involves honestly being willing to give up our grudges, big and small. Over the years, we accumulate a staggering number of them. Setting aside dedicated periods for healing practices is highly beneficial. Make a practice of wiping the mental slate clean every night. Treat each person as a fresh meeting and respond accordingly. In this way, you will slowly delete the poison that has amassed in your system. Remember, the poison is targeting you, so getting rid of it is greatly in your interest.

A helpful aid in viewing everyone compassionately is to see them as part of your family. When someone is mean, how would you respond if they were your loved sibling? You would understand the mental space they are coming from. If someone does something stupid or ignorant, how would you respond if they were your child? You would be concerned for them and do your best to help develop their understanding of life. No resentment required. No criticism needed. No hurt necessary.

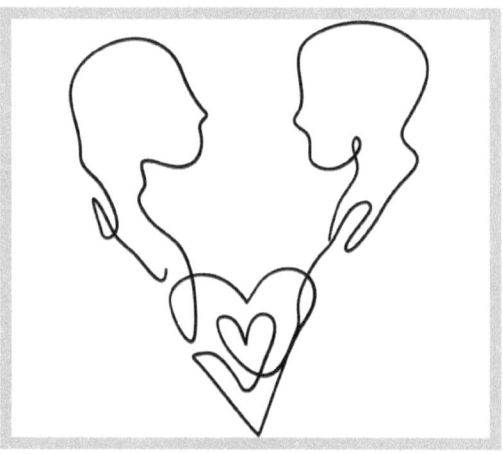

Most of what we do in forgiveness practices is burning up karma—our own and other people's. It's only difficult when we don't understand the tremendous and happy benefits of doing so.

True forgiveness is not sacrificing ourselves to someone else's nasty, destructive ways. It is not overlooking something bad because we are "benevolent and better." It's much more effective than that. It is understanding the dynamics of suffering. Ultimately, it is seeing the essential nature of spiritual existence where the concept of forgiveness becomes superfluous.

The more innocent we are, the more we see the world as innocent. The more riddled with hate we are, the more we see the world as hateful. Angry people always blame others and feel justified when they see an unsafe world. Loving people spread goodwill and feel the world is safe. So, as we go about our day, we should look at everyone as our friend and the whole world as our home.

I am a friend to the world.
The world is a friend to me.

CHAPTER 13

being liked

People commonly put much effort and worry into trying to be accepted and liked. Not only is it a waste of valuable energy, but it won't work. What will work is this:

1. **Accept** that some of your attempts to reach out to others won't work. That is okay. People are different. Not everyone will appreciate who you are, and some will have their own reasons for rejecting you. It doesn't matter. It's just the way life and people are.
2. Be your **authentic** inner self, the one that bubbles away in your deepest being. An irresistible radiance comes from people who are comfortable with themselves. Even if you are very different to others, your acceptance of yourself will help them to accept and appreciate you.
3. Don't **focus** on what other people think about you. Concentrate on what you think about others. Make your thoughts toward everyone well-

meaning, caring, understanding, and inclusive. And when people are snakish, simply and wisely move away. Then, forget about it. Don't stash it away in the cupboard of resentments. Keep that cupboard empty with open doors so the sweet air constantly moves through it.

CHAPTER 14

shining through

It was my first time living in an apartment. I was on the 9th floor facing east. The views of the sunrise were spectacular, and I could see the storms rolling in. However, I found it ungrounding to live so far above the ground and unearthing not to have some earth in the form of a garden.

This move was my third opportunity to downsize, and each time had been an extensive clearing. When you are raising a family, you acquire a lot of stuff. Much of it helps make a warm, interesting home for everyone. Being rather monkish by nature, I was happily taking very little this time. A few things are always our last material possessions to part with. They are usually worthless, but not to us. For mothers, they inevitably include special presents from children.

1. One item was a tea-light candle holder from my eldest son when he first went overseas at around twenty.
2. Another was a tea-light candle holder from my youngest son. It was his first present to me with his own money and thought. Boys must find tea-light candle holders to be economical mother-type presents.
3. A third item was a blue, stained-glass, half-moon mobile from my daughter, with her first paycheck at age fifteen. It cost half her wage. She got paid, went a few doors down, bought it, and proudly brought it home. Her economics has improved since then. It's called survival.
4. Another valued possession was a gift from my parents when I was twelve. It was glass bookends with an image of praying hands. Those days, most kids didn't have a lot. Families were bigger. Also, inexpensive, throwaway products weren't readily available. The few special things we had were treasured.

My friend said,
"The light shines through all the chosen items."

CHAPTER 15
our dearest friends

When my youngest son was twenty-four, he moved out of home. He was already living independently within the apartment—paying his share of the rent, shopping, and cooking for himself. Regardless, moving out is a big step because the young adult is moving away from their emotional base (hopefully). At that age, and as a male with the particular personality he has, I felt that I needed to set up a regular contact point, or he could drift out into the world a little anchorless. I suggested that we meet for lunch once a week at a cafe he liked (but didn't like so much that a mother would be uncool), and, as an added enticement, I would pay. After a few months, I upped the ante by suggesting we take turns paying. Still acceptable—going well!

I try to talk about all the things that he's interested in and also things that I feel are good for his development. The focus is on him, but that doesn't necessarily mean it's about him. The focus is on what he needs for his happiness and wellbeing. That could be me sharing things about my life so that he gets the opportunity to care and be a problem solver. Apart from that, there is a genuine sense of enjoying each other's company. If we want our adult children to like and respect us, we must treat them with the love, admiration, and respect we would our dearest friends—because they are.

It is a privilege to have young people in our lives (when we are not young) and close contact with people who are different to us. We can learn so much from them. It gives us access to information about the world that otherwise could slip past us as the years go on. It's important to stay connected to the world and not feel that we don't understand or can't keep up with it. If we don't keep moving, we will get left behind. If we don't move our body right till it stops, it will stop prematurely. If we don't use our mind, it will atrophy. If we don't keep our emotions alive, they will hide in fear. If we don't keep living a full, active, engaged life, then life will lose interest in us.

CHAPTER 16
way, wayward, and wayless

As my youngest son is a part-time musician and I am a writer, we often exchange thoughts and experiences about the creative process. To be authentic in our creations, we must share what comes from our personal experiences and individual makeup. For him, that involves a lot of fire, passion, and intensity—the raw, base-like energy that rightly belongs to many young males.

"Maybe it's too intense," he said after one of his song releases. "I don't want to be destructive."

"It's empowering," I said. "Think of a girl your age who might need to leave a destructive relationship. Listening to it could give her the burn to fire up and leave that boyfriend. Or a sportsperson. They need lots of bass-level energy. It's fine. Do what comes naturally to you. It will soon enough change into something else. You might as well use it to the max while it's there."

"Empowering is better than destructive," he said.

"We're all different," I said. "We can't have a world full of people like me."

He agreed that we definitely didn't need a world full of

people like me. I can fire up if I have to protect something or someone, but my preference is for peace. You shouldn't fight yourself. You should make your natural state work for you in the direction you want to travel.

If you have fire,
use it to ignite and light.

If you have heart,
heal the heartless and heartbroken.

If you have humour,
make the world brighter and better.

If you have insight,
show the way for the wayward and wayless.

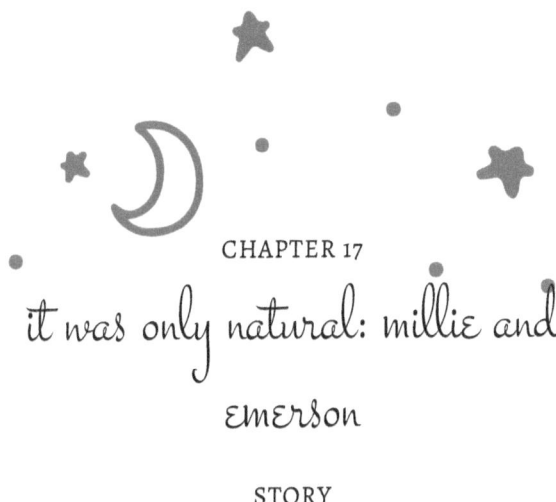

CHAPTER 17

it was only natural: millie and emerson

STORY

Emerson was a man who didn't cry about himself. He cried at the movies, but that was about other people's lives. He was used to carrying on with his responsibilities. However, on this particular day, he was sobbing.

Millie hugged him and said, "I'm so sorry, Emerson. We have been friends for so long. I know you want us to be together, but I feel we are better as friends."

Although apologetic for crying, Emerson kept crying. After many years of weariness in his personal life, he finally had the opportunity to be with someone he wanted. He also knew that to move into the next stage of his life, he would need to change many things, and those around him wouldn't like it. Courage wasn't his strong point. He was good. He wasn't brave. Millie said she would help him as a friend, but he felt it would not be enough. He was probably right. He loved Millie, but more than that, he needed her. He was so close to getting what he wanted, but her answer was still no.

Millie and Emerson didn't take long to start talking again after the difficult discussion about being friends, not lovers. They had been friends for so many years that it was only natural to talk again. They returned to seeing each other as much as before, if not more. Millie didn't say no to Emerson again. She let the couple relationship happen. He was a good man. He deserved the help. The relationship was easily compatible. They were both easy to live with. However, the worth of a relationship is not based on ease but on purpose and depth.

Emerson came from a controlling family and community. Were they controlling? Not really. They were just ordinary people. Anyone can become a tyrant if we let them. Even the most inoffensive of dogs can become a monster in their home if their master becomes a servant to them, afraid to take the lead.

Emerson owned just such a tyrant dog—a little Maltese called Poppet. The dog had been a lone and loved canine member of her family for twelve years. To mention a few problems—she would bite anyone whenever it suited her, refuse to eat anything but what she fancied at the moment, would not go through the dog flap unless someone opened it for her, and would sleep on whichever bed she wished to, biting the bed occupant's feet if they dared to move in a way which annoyed her. With all the pampering, fussing, and loving, she was a mental mess. She would shake uncontrollably at everything and nothing. She was depressed and anxious and would alienate herself from humans by barking at and biting anyone she did not trust, which was pretty much everyone. As for her relationship with other dogs? Dogs? "There are no dogs but me. I do not even see them."

LOVE MATTERS

Is spoiling someone (or some dog) love? No, it creates problem after problem for those who live the illusion that life rotates around them and that they are entitled. Many well-meaning dog owners are big on loving the dog first. If you tell them that dogs need rules, many people believe it will hurt their dog. Dogs need you to be the pack leader. Millie and Poppet had world-class battles for the head of the pack position. Eventually, Poppet surrendered, and her anxiety and depression disappeared.

At every turn, the "tyrants" in Emerson's family and community were challenged—not by Emerson but by Millie. Millie knew that if she didn't stand her ground, not only would Emerson remain imprisoned, but she would become the next victim once she was committed to the relationship. As soon as one tyrant was put in its place, another appeared. It only took a little while for all the would-be tyrants to join forces to try and recapture their lost territory. For many reasons, people can become allies to face a supposed enemy. People will fight hard not to lose whatever they got from previously captured territory. Eventually, the enemies retreated. Emerson relaxed, thought the battle was over, and congratulated himself on doing a good job. That was a fatal mistake. The enemy bided their time, regrouped, and came in with a new approach. If you cannot win by insults, you can often win by compliments. Compliments can do what insults cannot. That was the beginning of the end.

They were not tough battles for Millie. On her own, she could have handled them quickly. A *no*, which means *no*, is a formidable defence in any situation. However, she wasn't on her own. When one helps another to fight their battles, the problem is generally not the thing that is opposed, but the person one is helping to stand their ground. Emerson would unwittingly open a door and two windows for every secured house. If we are good but not strong, we must learn that, without courage, other people will destroy our life. Everything we value is open to being taken or destroyed by a stronger person. We must know how to defend ourselves, our truth, our gifts, and what is precious to us. We mustn't open the doors and windows to thieves of happiness. Emerson loved Millie as much as he could love any woman. He loved her, but he loved his safety more.

When Millie felt Emerson could bear to hear it, she said, "If you cannot protect yourself, how can you ever protect me? You will let them destroy us rather than own your truth."

Self-preservation kicked in, and Millie left. She and Emerson remained good friends. They had been friends so long. It was only natural.

CHAPTER 18

how did he ever find you: amy and mervin

STORY

The Manhattan hairdresser asked with genuine intrigue, "But, darling, how did your husband, Mervin, ever find you in Australia?" Amy could see that he envisaged Mervin setting off from the States on a quest to find his wife-to-be and, against all odds, finding her amongst the wild kangaroos of outback Australia. There was more than a bit of truth in it.

Mervin was everything Amy was not—sophisticated, wealthy, and worldly. If it had not been for his mid-life crisis and a conscientious effort to find a spiritual path, neither would have come into contact with the other. After significant professional success and a few failed marriages, Mervin decided that a move to Australia would be an opportunity to find a new direction in life. He was serious in his quest. A swift and sharp intellect guaranteed he read every trailblazing spiritual and psychological book on the market. After friending young Amy at a spiritual meeting, they found that they shared a love of deep thinking and literature.

Amy's first visit to Mervin's apartment was pivotal. It wasn't because of a passionate love affair. It was more of a love affair with his books. As Amy walked hesitantly into his lavish hallway, she stopped in her tracks at the rows of beautiful books lining the wall. All the books she had ever wanted to read were right there—the time-honoured wisdom of the spiritual masters, the work of the founding psychologists, the new thought of the mind-pioneers, the inspiration of the mystic poets, and the classic sacred texts. When Amy was a young teenager, she often went into the Christian bookshop on the way home from school. She didn't have enough money to buy even one book in all the time she went there. She told herself that, one day, she would have enough money to buy hundreds of books.

Amy felt that she had found a spiritual and intellectual soulmate in Mervin. And Mervin thought he had found a real chance to have a loving family in Amy. Kind, nurturing, and intelligent, she was a true find. As she was young, she had little baggage from life. He believed they could start from scratch and create the family life he longed for. As life would have it, Mervin's mid-life honesty and commitment lasted only a few short years. Although Amy had found Mervin at the right moment in his life, she did not realise that it was but a moment and a long way from being sustainable for him.

Nevertheless, the relationship turned Amy into a woman. It gave her life experience, culture, a new language, and a more sophisticated way of speaking. It gave her an understanding of wealth, so she knew it would never be necessary to feel less than anyone. She could handle money if it came her way and not chase it if it did not. She had lived in a world much older than herself, which changed her. It made her older than her years. Despite its long, drawn-out, and lonely demise, the relationship had blessed her. It was a blessing, but more of a blessing when it was over.

PART THREE

mystic matters

HEALING AND SPIRITUAL HAPPINESS

CHAPTER 19

spotlights

SPIRITUAL PATH

EXISTENCE AND CONSCIOUSNESS

BROADENED BOUNDARIES

As humans, we have a natural, inbuilt desire to constantly grow and expand our inner boundaries.

CENTRE OF UNIVERSE

Think of yourself as the centre of the universe—not in a selfish way, but in a way that reminds you that you have the power to create your thoughts. Your thoughts have the power to create your world. If this is true, which it is, then you have the power to change your thoughts and make your world a beautiful one.

CONSCIOUSNESS

Although people feel that their fear and anxiety are specific to particular experiences, they come from a general unsettled and unaware consciousness. The more we lift our state of being, the less fear and anxiety we will have.

AWAKE OR ASLEEP

Awake or asleep, we have two companions: the relentless, restless personal mind and the divine Mind. Choose carefully whom you will allow such intimate and influential access.

SELF-HELP

There is no need to try and "love yourself" when you realise that you are made from love and live in love. There is no need to try and motivate yourself when you don't want to waste your beautiful life. There is no need to try and forgive someone who hurt you when you don't want the burden of blame. Self-help can be helpful, but once we connect with life's Source, we don't need to help our "self." The entire force of creation effortlessly, brilliantly, and compassionately carries that self.

ABSOLUTELY ALIVE

It's of the utmost importance that we make the most of our time on Earth. It is the fragile nature of life that makes being here so valuable. Every day is a tremendous opportunity.

TRULY TRUE

We should question all our beliefs and assumptions because otherwise, we can end up living a life that is not truly ours or truly true.

MY MIND

My state of mind is MY responsibility.

SPECIAL TO THE DIVINE

> *You are special to the Divine.*
> *You have a purpose*
> *and fulfilling that purpose*
> *will make you happy.*
> *You are loved and you are safe.*

> *The life you have been given is*
> *a wonderful opportunity to*
> *learn, grow, heal, and*
> *become a fully functioning,*
> *happy, and magnificent creation.*

FOR SURE

"What are three things about life you know for sure?"

1. God loves me. The Divine energy loves me.
2. God loves you. God. Loves. You.
3. Life is precious.

EVERY LIFE

Every life and every lifeform is as intricate and marvellous as our own. The increasing realisation of this is an indication of developing consciousness.

CARE

The world's greatest need is for care. The more evolved we become as a collective world, the more caring we will become about each other and our planet.

PEACE

Peace is a sense of sure stability. It's not something that we can do. It's a being. We become more open to the peace around us, in us, and through us. We become more in touch with the spiritual domain, which is innately peaceful.

PRAY AWAY

It's important that we pray for our family and friends. As spiritual seekers, we consider the whole world as family and friends. However, we also have our own personal connections. The energy you create when you pray for someone can change their lives. For instance, many mothers have saved the lives of their children in dire situations simply by their prayers.

AIRTIME

Don't give negative thoughts and entities airtime. The only power they have is the power of your attention. Gently but firmly redirect your thoughts in the direction you truly wish to go, which is your happiness and wholeness.

GOD

We can talk about God endlessly, but only by experiencing the Source do we start to know the Divine. It's something that must be *experienced*.

MIND CONTROL

We do not have control over many external things, but we can control our own mind. We can refuse to be befuddled and cloudy. We can be clear, intentional, kind, strong, and expectant. Once we decide that is how we want our mind to be, we will get much invisible help to keep us on track as it is not just for our benefit but for everyone around us.

MIND AND FEAR

Our mind makes fear, and it can also reassure us that there is nothing to fear. We can make the mind work for us, not against us. We need to take control of our wandering thoughts. We are cared for by the force that blew existence into us. The mind aligned with God has an enormous and extraordinary power to heal itself and be a healing channel for others, much of which we will never even know about.

LOVE TAKES CARE OF COURAGE

When you allow the love of Life to flow through you, there is no need to try and be brave. Love takes care of courage. It sees nothing to be afraid of. It sees beauty and security in this temporary life and the One that continuously nurtures it.

GUILT

Prolonged and accumulated guilt is neither a virtue nor a helpful self-growth tool. It is a defence against growth, an excuse not to grow. It is, in essence, self-pity. There is a big difference between prolonged guilt and facing one's mistakes in order to correct them. Once we see faults as mistakes, not inherent badness, it is relatively easy to take the next step and not make the same mistake again.

PERSONAL FEAR

Say to yourself:

> *I do not allow my thoughts to revolve around my personal fears.*
> *I am here for God, and that is all.*
>
> *God cares about everyone and everything and that's what I do.*
>
> *God will look after me, so I don't have to worry about myself.*

INTENSITY

If you can create intense negative feelings in yourself, you can also create intense positive feelings. Intensity is a gift. With the right teaching, willingness, perseverance, and enthusiasm, it can be used to make a magnificent, meaningful life.

ENERGY AND EVOLUTION

PLACE TO START

If you want to change the outer aspects of your life, you need to change the inner.

GIFT GIVE

If you have a gift—any type of gift, something you love—by nature of the fundamentals of existence, there are people who need that gift. So relax, share what you love without stress, and the natural balance of need for what you have will be drawn to you.

TEACHABILITY

The less people know, the more arrogant they tend to be. Someone who is very teachable in any field realises that there is an endless amount they don't know. The masters are innately teachable.

DEFENCE

The make-up of ordinary human consciousness is to be heavily defended against life's truths. It helps to say to oneself:

1. I have a lot to learn, but that is okay. I wouldn't be here if I didn't have much to learn.
2. I make many mistakes. I make them all the time, but that is alright. I wouldn't be here if I didn't make many mistakes.
3. No matter how many mistakes I make or what I understand or don't, I am intrinsically and

completely loved and appreciated by the Life that created me. That very life is trying to pull me forward. It is safe to follow, even if I feel that I am following in the dark.

GENTLE, GRACIOUS, GRATEFUL

It is not necessary to learn our life lessons painfully. We can learn them gently, graciously, and with happy gratitude that we were wrong and that there is a better way.

SABOTAGE

If you are trying to follow your dreams and passions but, somehow, you keep sabotaging yourself, then one part of you is working against another part. An outright battle will do no good. Instead, make a compromise with yourself. Make a deal with the anxious, fearful, unconvinced part of you that you will give just a little room for the inspired part of you to flourish with freedom. When it works (which it will), you will, little by little, be convinced that the whole thing is safe. You will train yourself not to be anxious and to trust your intuitive being.

BEST OPTION

The more we think it is up to us to protect and create our life, the more fear we will have. The more we see that the One Life protects and guides our every moment and movement, the calmer and more creative we will be. Humility, as an acknowledgement of truth, is the only sensible and viable option.

I DON'T KNOW

If you want to get rid of your suffering, you must be ready to move to a different understanding of life and a higher stage of development. If you are not prepared to say that you do not currently know, no matter how much the Divine wants to help you, it will not go against your wishes. Despite the suffering involved, it respects your individuality and right to live as you choose. Be humble and open your heart and mind to receive what will make you well, happy, and a blessing beyond your belief.

LEANINGS AND LOVES

So many of the difficulties in life come from not being who we truly are. It seems so simple, but not many people do it. Trust yourself. Trust your divine nature, which is inherent in every single person. Trust that you can follow your natural, individual leanings and loves, and you will have a wonderful, creative, and inspired life beyond what you can currently even perceive.

PATHWAY

Think of those times when you were at your best—your most balanced, productive, alive, humorous, intelligent, caring, and capable self. Aim to expand those moments so that they last longer and are more frequent. They are your path indicator.

EXCITING NEWS

When unpleasant things happen, consider them fantastic learning opportunities. When we approach everything like this, nothing is overly painful or damaging. We say, "I'm using this for my personal growth because there is something important for me to learn in this situation." Then, it's even exciting! We know we're going to benefit from it.

POINTS OF CHANGE

As our consciousness evolves, we progress from one concept of ourselves to another, each having increased truth, depth, and peace of mind. The most difficult places are often the points of change. We know the old has been outgrown, but we do not yet fully grasp the new. Do not fear. The Spirit is gentle and sure. Spread your wings, knowing that you are riding on Divine air currents.

PAIN'S PURPOSE

If you are in a large amount of nonspecific mental or energetic pain, it is one of two things. You are either functioning worse than the average person (who is in pain but at a more tolerable level), or you are preparing for the next stage of your evolution, and the one you are currently in is becoming unbearable. If you are reading this, it is the latter rather than the former. So, take heart, keep going, be very careful what you absorb into your consciousness, and look for teachers who can really help you and make a significant difference. Your next stage of life understanding will bring you much peace and fulfilment. It's absolutely worth the struggle.

COMFORT AND CHALLENGE

When it comes to spiritual teachings, if we reach for what feels comfortable and aligned with our state of being, then we won't grow much. We have to reach for what challenges us and comes from a higher place than where we currently are. If you are not sure, then look at the teacher. Is the teacher's life "better" than yours? Do they have more capacity for insight, love, angerlessness, compassion, serenity, healing, intelligence, creativity, and usefulness? If so, then follow that way.

DELICIOUS

Don't try to dispose of painful emotions such as grief, sadness, fury, despair, and terror. Think of them as ingredients for making a spectacular meal. If you combine and cook them in just the right way, a lot of karma will burn up and evaporate in the process, and you'll create something delicious.

ON YOUR SIDE

Every situation in life carries pain of some sort. It's an inbuilt part of the life experience. Don't try to avoid pain, or you will shut life out. Your world will get smaller and smaller, and your fear will get greater and greater. Throw yourself into life despite its difficulties, trusting you can navigate it with wisdom. Life is on your side when you desire to bless, not hurt.

PEACE GUIDE

Your guide is peace. To return to the happy way of peace, you must be willing to acknowledge that you do not know what you are doing. That allows the Divine to guide you. It will always guide you aright.

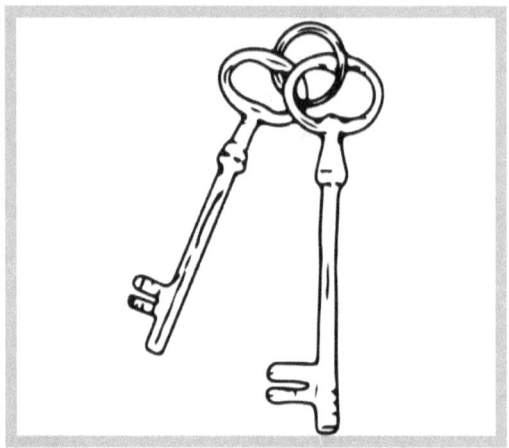

WORKING WELL

We have to have faith that the design of this most magnificent system of life is to have it work well, easily, and perfectly in us.

FLAT LINING

If you feel a bit down, you could be moving into a different stage of your life. A dream, a new direction, may be trying to emerge. Before it reformulates properly, some aspect of the old will have to die.

PARTINGS

Some partings are necessary for new growth. You have to let go of one thing to create something else. It doesn't necessarily mean that you are permanently leaving behind the previous thing. It may be that you are leaving behind the format it took. If the leaves did not let go of their trees in autumn and fall to the ground, there would be no spring.

INTERNAL MAP

Everyone is born with an internal map of how to navigate this life best according to their capabilities, evolution, and leanings. Look at your map often to ensure you are headed where you genuinely want to go.

UNIQUE FUNCTION

You have a unique and special function to fulfil. Your life is of the highest importance and value to the Divine and those around you. Dedicate yourself wholeheartedly to improving yourself so that your gift to the world will expand along with your happiness.

WORTHY

It is never a matter of being *worthy* or *unworthy* of God's love. God loves us—end of story. Worth is not a consideration. Anyway, you are automatically worthy because God only makes quality.

PEACE-BRINGER

Tell yourself that you are a peace-bringer. Come what may, you are here to love, heal, comfort, and awaken. You are a part of God—endlessly valued and throbbing with creative energy.

TRUST

If you are on the spiritual path, you must trust that it is much more than your own small intentions. The path itself will guide and support you and show you what is best for you. Trust the path, your guides, the Divine, and the drive that put you on the path in the first place.

WAY IN

If you wholeheartedly want to absorb a teaching, don't use your thinking mind (for example, don't take notes in a teaching situation). Let it find its own way in and become a part of you.

LINKING IT

You must learn to connect your thoughts with your suffering. Then, you will become intensely interested in alternative thoughts, energies, and behaviours. Progress will be sporadic, unpredictable, and painful without a clear understanding of the link.

TRANSCENDENCE

Energy knows neither space nor time. That is why you can always call on a teacher's help whether they are living or not, near or far, personally aware of you or not, busy or quiet.

SAME, SAME

We all want the same things—happiness, fearlessness, fulfilment, peace, enrichment, love, health, and aliveness.

SACRED SPACES

Like people, places have their own unique energy. If we understand and respect that, we can use them for our growth.

SPIRITUAL PRACTICES

FACELESS

Our body has a face, but our mind does not. Practice seeing yourself and others as faceless manifestations of energy. Rather than making your world dark and desolate, it will enliven your whole life experience as boundless and brilliantly exciting.

THAT IS ME

A practice that can help reduce and eliminate comparative thinking is to see yourself in everyone. If someone does something good, we say, "That is me." If someone does something bad, we say, "That is me." Something embarrassing, "That is me." Something magnificent, "That is me." If we are part of other people, we will not feel jealous, ill-willed, prideful or any other distasteful emotion stemming from comparative thinking.

WAY WE DO IT

It's not what we do but how we do it that makes the most difference in our own and others' lives.

WIDER RESPONSIBILITY

As we evolve, the scope of our responsibility widens. That does not mean that we have endless things to do. It means we look at everything with concern, compassion, and a willingness to do whatever is appropriate and possible for us.

ENDLESSLY FASCINATING

You can make anything into a spiritual practice by becoming conscious of your inner world. Whatever you happen to be doing on the outside, if you connect the outward with the inward, you will become conscious. It gives you perspective—a step away from being blindly immersed in your body's reactions and mind's compulsive thoughts. You will never again be bored because living "awake" is endlessly fascinating.

ENDLESS ALTERNATIVES

The faulty alternatives to spiritual growth are endless. Must we try all of them? The driving force of our evolution is either suffering or wisdom. As we develop, there is less suffering and more wisdom. The pull of wisdom becomes greater.

RECONSTRUCTION

A spiritual teacher is no teacher if they do not have the energetic ability to reconstruct your internal world. That is not a comfortable process because it dissolves ways of seeing that we are attached to. The great saving grace is that every step brings a more beautiful personal reality.

DE-STRESS DON'T DISTRESS

Putting aside dedicated time for spiritual practices is the way to de-stress, refocus, gain peace of mind, gather your intention, find your direction, regain your health, and come upon inspiration.

MOMENT-BY-MOMENT PRACTICE

Expecting to get through your day without some outer or inner problems is unrealistic. That is why our mental and spiritual practices are so vital and helpful. Throughout the day, keep reorienting your inner compass in the direction you are trying to go. Read little sentences from books or social media that inspire you and keep you on track. Repeat phrases in your mind that lift you and stop you from worrying. Don't allow yourself to drown in misery. Happiness is not a once-and-for-all occurrence. It's a moment-by-moment practice. As with all practices, it gets easier with conscious repetition.

CHECK IN

Wherever you go, whatever you do, remember to check in with your inner self. And if you can, stay checked in. You are not your body. Nor are you your mind. You are much more, far greater, infinitely more beautiful, resilient, and marvellous.

MEDITATIVE MIND

To have a meditative mind does not necessarily mean to sit cross-legged and AUM. It is more a matter of disarming the egoic mind, which goes on and on uselessly. If we find the mind settles in nature, then that is a good place to naturally become meditative. There are many other places where this can happen as well. The point is to become calm and peaceful so that your whole system, including your body, can settle and realign. The more often you do this, the more meditative you will become.

WANDER AND WONDER

In spiritual practices, we enlarge the sphere of our mind. We should give enough time for our mind to wander and wonder, venture into the unknown, play with creative thoughts, and dance with "boredom".

ACCEPTANCE

The starting point of getting rid of worry is acceptance. Accept the problem for what it is. Fighting demons in the dark creates a lot of stress and anxiety. Sit or lie quietly and see the tension in your stomach area. Don't try to eliminate it. See it, breathe into it, let it be, and absorb it into your system. In this way, you are handing it to Life. You will start to see it in a new light, that of the Greater Power, which is safe, serene, intelligent, and entirely responsive.

JOY'S WAY

Whenever you feel afraid, say to yourself,

> *"Joy is my way,
> and that is all."*

LEARNING TO BE NOTHING

People often say they would like to learn meditation and think it can be used for their benefit. It *is* for their benefit, but not in the way they normally assume. For meditation to be truly beneficial, we have to enter it with the thought of nothingness —that we want nothing and are nothing. All our somethingness can be taken up again later, but we will find that we do not reacquire it with such great enthusiasm.

DIRECTION NOT DESPAIR

Whenever you despair about the world, tell yourself that you will have made this world a little better by the time you die.

HEALING

Healing is reaching an equilibrium in our consciousness where grace is present. Grace is peace, love, happiness, and joy.

LOOSEN THE FEAR

A great deal of sickness comes from repressed anger that gets lodged in the body. If you loosen the anger, you will see that it is based on fear. If you loosen the fear, you will see that it is a mistake. It is a mistaken concept of life and safety. Therein lies healing.

DON'T RESIST

If you want something to heal—physical, environmental, emotional—you must first accept it for what it is. Don't resist it. Don't blame yourself for not knowing better already. Accept it without judgment. You'll find that genuinely accepting the present situation allows it to change much more rapidly than otherwise.

TRANSFER OF ENERGY

The transfer of healing is energetic, not through words. That is why we feel better around certain people and worse around others. Try to make your presence beneficial—one that will benefit you, everyone you interact with, and all you think of.

HANG UP

Don't let fear hijack you. Acknowledge it, but as you would an unwanted marketing phone call, say, "I'm not interested," and hang up.

PRACTICE OF PRESENCE

When we are in pain, our thoughts become more centred on our personal existence, which is an experiential disaster. We need to get our thoughts away from our personal self and allow the realisation of our complete safety to replace the mounting fear. We are part of God. Our purpose here is to shine a light of love. That's the way for us to feel safe and happy. We surrender to God's care. That's the whole of it. God, thankfully, does the rest.

TURNING ATTENTION

The best way to reduce anxiety and fear is to become a place for the expression of love. Love takes many forms. It doesn't matter which form you use—warmth, practical assistance, community service in any of its myriad varieties, humour, entertainment, education, inspiration, any contribution to the world's well-being, doing your job with a smile, or heartfulness. The mere act of turning our attention from ourselves to the outside world takes care of fear and anxiety.

SHAKE IT OFF

Make a conscientious practice of shaking off everything you are holding onto. Tell yourself that you are a continuously renewing lifeform. This way, your body and energy body will be a fresh, vital entity available to a full range of opportunities, experiences, and grace.

MANTRA

A mantra to heal worry:

> *I am here to be a healing presence.*

SHADOWS

Do not be afraid of the shadows you brought with you. They slink around, jump out and scare you, and sometimes decide to stay for extended periods. If you did not have shadows, you would not be here. Patiently and wholeheartedly give them to the Divine, whose light makes a happy place where shadows disappear.

EVER-EVOLVING

Do not accept your limitations, frailties, and shortcomings as inevitable and unchangeable. See yourself as an ever-evolving being, moving towards perfect physical and mental health, spiritual equanimity, and love.

BELIEF

You only "believe" in things that you don't really believe in. You have a doubt about their absolute validity. When you experience something as a fundamental reality, there is no need for belief. It is when people "believe" that they get offended by others who don't believe the same thing. When you know something to be true, it doesn't matter what someone else sees or doesn't see. The reality of something is not offended, changed, or dissipated in the slightest by someone else's belief or non-belief in it.

SPONTANEOUS HEALING

Healings happen naturally and spontaneously when we align our thinking and awareness with the energetic reality around us. However, we cannot and should not try to direct them. Our job is to see. The Divine does the "fixing" with an intelligence and love beyond ours. We can be assured that all is well when a grateful, harmonious calm has settled in our consciousness. Our seeing frees others to, likewise, see.

SMALL AND SPECIFIC

Rather than set your spiritual and personal goals too high, have small, daily, realistic, specific ones that are achievable and will have a cumulative effect on your growth.

For instance, don't say, "I won't get angry anymore." Say something like, "Today, when I get upset about little things, I will stop, breathe, and remind myself that I can manage this without becoming an emotional rollercoaster."

Another example is instead of saying, "I won't gossip anymore," say something like, "The next time I'm in a conversation when I hear myself or someone else relaying damaging, possibly untrue, humorous at-their-expense information about another person, I will stop and ask myself if this is really going to add to my long-term well-being."

BECOMING MINDLESS

A highly helpful practice is to stop having so many opinions. The conventional mind has opinions about everything and everyone. You may think it's easy to let your opinions go. If so, it's because you haven't done it. Try it as a practice. Next time you catch yourself rolling along on a thought train of opinionatedness about something or someone, stop. If you can't, tell yourself that you will put your opinions down just for five minutes. You'll be amazed at how freeing it is. Oh, the freedom of not having such an important mind!

MANAGING MIND

If we cannot manage our own mind, we will never be able to craft life the way we want it. Meditation is the fastest way to access and develop mind control.

PRESENT PRESENCE

If we want to be a healing presence, we must be present. Our attention must be focused on the wholeness, happiness, and beauty of life in its purity. Undivided attention to spiritual reality helps everything to align with that.

ONLY LOVE

Fill your heart with love. See your heart as being full of love. Have love for everyone you come across and feel that everyone has love for you. Make sure that love extends from you to your family members, extended family, friends, enemies, work colleagues, and fellow inhabitants of Earth. In your heart, there is only love.

NO SHADOW

We don't have to stress about what other people do—their ignorance, jealousy, lack of love, anger, malice, and the mess in their heads. They generally don't know what they're doing. Make sure your head and heart are clear. Don't let the shadow of lovelessness fall on you.

KARMA BURNING

Most people don't burn up their current karma; they collect more. However, when we become committed to the spiritual path, we start burning. We can't burn it up all at once as it would be overwhelming. Imagine the worst thing that has happened in your current life and multiply it countless times from other existences. No, that would be too much. Our soul knows how to best burn the karma—sometimes, in chunks, sometimes little by little. And your spiritual teachers burn it for you. The more evolved the teacher is, the more karma they can handle for you. Trust the burning process. It has an intelligence of indescribable accuracy and relevancy.

KICKING KARMA

People carry much more karma than they realise. Not all karma is bad; some is good. When karma is heavy and unconscious, it will affect your life through illness, mental restlessness, relationship problems, and spiritual blockages. We want to gradually reduce and replace it with stable, strong energy systems.

STEAM OFF WATER

Past mistakes, unpleasant situations, things that didn't go well, and unfortunate decisions create karma. Encourage them to drift out of your body and etheric body like steam coming off boiling water. We don't have to keep thinking about these things—there are so many. We want a clean foundation. Ask the invisible entities to help you. They will.

GOD GOES WITH ME

If we keep in our hearts and minds that God goes with us wherever we go, it helps with every single moment of life. If we keep to our spiritual practices, then gently and gradually, our ego will have less and less hold on us. Our energetic state will become more extensive, calmer, and more capable. Doors will open for us. The drive towards God and our spiritual evolution will become stronger. There will be no question of going back. What would we go back to? Misery? Problems? We want to go forward.

JUST A MINUTE

Sometimes, you only have a minute (or can only tolerate a minute) for your spiritual practices. It's okay. A minute can save you. Other times, you can settle into a proper session. Your body and mind generally need at least twenty minutes to attain a meditative, beneficial state. However, even a minute will make a world of difference in helping you relax, disengage from your worries, and connect with your Divine nature.

UNIMPORTANT

No matter how "important" your doings become, remember to do "unimportant" things with the same enthusiasm. It's humbling, grounding, enlivening, innocent, and fun. We are all unimportant in the grand scheme of things. Yet, we are also of immense and unique value to the structure of life.

DEVOTION

Devotion means dissolution. We dissolve ourselves into what we are devoted to. It is how we lose ourselves and also how we find ourselves. It is both powerless and ultimately powerful.

DISSOLUTION

The path to enlightenment is paved with self-dissolution. What self wants that? No self would want it. No self would trust it. However, if one perseveres, the beauty, capacity, and trouble-free nature of spiritual life gain a hold. It is realised that ease and happiness are lost whenever the small self is in command. Generally, it is a gradual process of seeing that everything beautiful and worthy comes from allowing the spiritual force to live in us, and everything fragile, ugly, and unreliable comes from our persistent delusions.

ENLIGHTENMENT

The steps of spiritual progression are complex and varied. Enlightenment is not a black-and-white affair. It is a doorway, the end of common suffering. Once through the door, there is infinite room for growth. Enlightenment can be the smiling, quietly-knowing type passed on from a capable master to a receptive and humble student or the type that belongs to a guru capable of changing the world. It lights the person up inside and removes the rotating field of endless suffering humans otherwise experience. In essence, the enlightened individual moves into an unshakeable field of happiness that remains regardless of the ups and downs of life.

OUTER FROM THE INNER

When you focus on your inner world,
you forget about your body,
age, history, parents, relationships,
children, home, and employment.

It is an entirely inward process.
Your soul is nameless, bodiless,
relationshipless, and jobless.
You have come from the Great Beyond.

It is a privilege to be here.
You want to make the most of it
and form the happy outer
from the sweet inner.

CHAPTER 20

healing

HELPFUL OR HAYWIRE

KEVIN AND THE CANINES

On a late afternoon walk along the creek near my house, I saw a man sitting at one of the picnic tables in the distance. He was alone and resting his head in his hands. He looked very gloomy.

I wish he weren't so sad, I thought. *There's no need to be. If only he knew that.*

I felt there was nothing else I could do, so I continued walking. However, as I drew closer, I realised he had five puppies in a portable pen on the grass.

"Is it okay for me to approach the puppies," I asked.

Surprised but pleased, he looked up and said, "Yes."

We had a little chat for about ten minutes. His name was Kevin, and he had driven from a small country town near Wagga Wagga, five hours north. He stopped in my little town for a break before the rest of the trip to the city, where the puppies would meet their new owners. Kevin said he was seventy-two years old. He was the sort of person who probably had never been married and likely had few friends, if any. He seemed rather reclusive, not because he was like a monk but because he didn't like people, only dogs.

Kevin proudly showed me Mum, Nannie, and Aunty, who were in travelling cages in the van. They all travelled together whenever he went anywhere. As the conversation drew to a close, he told me that his town now had 4,000 residents. Normally, he moved when his town got too big for him. However, he wouldn't be moving this time.

"This will be my last house and my last town," he said.

"Why?" I asked.

"I had cancer about a year ago," he said. "After treatment, I got better, but now I am having a cancer problem again in a different area. I start treatment in a week, for ten days."

He stopped talking but wordlessly conveyed that he thought his beloved dogs would soon be orphans. When someone tells you their life is about to end, you don't say something trite. It's the most precious thing they have.

"I have to go now," I said. "But I want you to know that starting next week, I will pray for you every day for ten days."

Kevin was not the kind of man you tell such a thing to. He was somewhat gruff, a bit rough, a country fella who probably had minimal education and limited contact with the wider world. He looked like he didn't have a religious bone in his body. But when you are desperate and desperately sad, any confidence that anyone sincerely has in your well-being and happiness is a lifeline. When you are sinking fast, with no help in sight, someone else's belief that all will be well (in whatever form that wellness will proceed) is a friend. He didn't scoff. He didn't say anything. He just stared at me with eyes that said, *I wish something could help me.*

"You are not as alone as you think," I said. "Please know that there are many invisible people around you who care about you."

He smiled as I waved goodbye. Not a smile that said, *She's a kind but delusional woman.* A smile that said, *For some strange reason, I have a feeling inside me that I do not understand. A feeling in my core telling me that, one way or another, I will be alright.*

When I got home, I felt a deep sense of contentment for Kevin, myself, and everyone else. I would never see Kevin again. I would never know what happened to him. But I didn't need to know. I could tell that something very real touched him. At a critical time, he was able to let a voice (that had been trying to speak to him for seventy-two years) tell him:

> *You are not alone.*
> *You are loved,*
> *and you are safe.*

HAYWIRE HEALING

In contrast to this recent beautiful experience with Kevin, I must tell you about another attempt at healing that went haywire when I was twenty-five. I was driving home with my then-husband and baby. I remember it was raining very heavily in our harbour-side Sydney suburb. When we were almost home, we saw a senior man lying on the pavement with a woman looking frantic and an abandoned umbrella erratically moving in the wind. I got out of the car to help.

The woman was the man's daughter. He had collapsed, and she was frantically trying to ring an ambulance. It was before mobile phones. She was knocking on people's doors, but no one answered. It was hard enough to even get into the properties as this was a wealthy area with high security. I told the woman that I would stay with her father while she kept trying. My husband went home with our baby and said he would ring an ambulance from our house.

I was left alone with the dead man and the madly screeching wind and rain. Somehow, amidst the noise of nature, it seemed still and quiet once everyone else had disappeared. I grabbed the umbrella as it was about to make a dash across the road. Even though the man and I were already soaked (and I don't think he cared either way), I held the umbrella over us.

I remembered a story I read a few days before. It was told by a person who had a miraculous healing.

> He had some sort of medical emergency (perhaps heart failure) while waiting for his train on the London Underground. He could recall the whole incident, even though he was no longer alive. He said that when he was lying on the ground, he saw a group of commuters gathering around him. A few ran to get help. Someone in the crowd quietly bent down to him and whispered in his ear, *God loves you.* He couldn't see who said it, but once said, something about the words changed his life, or death. The words crept into his dead body and brought him back to this world. He said to himself:
> *God loves me.*
> *Yes, God does love me.*
> *What am I doing lying on the ground?*
> *God loves me, so I need to get up.*
> He never knew who whispered the words in his ear, but they saved him.

Inspired by the story, I bent down to the dead man on the Sydney pavement and said to him, "God loves you."

Nothing.

"God loves you," I repeated.

Nothing.

It was probably getting annoying by now, and the dead man most likely wished me to shut up. He lay motionless on the hard, wet concrete, and I stood there staring sheepishly at my failed attempt to bring life to a lifeless body. The ambulance arrived and performed CPR. That didn't work either, but it was probably less annoying to the departing spirit.

Almost four decades later, as I sat in my home thinking about Kevin and the canines, I recalled the above incident with the dead man and the umbrella. What happened with Kevin was different. Not because I could do more after so many decades of spiritual work. It was because I knew how to do less. The entire communication with Kevin was orchestrated by the Divine. Yes, my heart reached out to him, sitting forlornly on the bench by the creek. But God showed me the puppies. God told me to go over. God told me what to say. And it was God's power that reached into Kevin's heart so that for, most likely, one of the rare times in his life, he had an experience of knowing he was loved and couldn't be alone. Everything wonderful comes from knowing that we are not alone and are surrounded by love.

*The most important thing about
healing is to remove ourselves.
We don't and can't do anything.
The whole thing is driven, inspired,
and executed by the Divine.*

*What we can do is not get in the way.
Also, we can listen.
And very importantly, we can care
enough about other people's suffering
that we want to help in the first place.*

PROFESSIONAL PRACTICE AS HEALER AND COUNSELLOR

I tried to start my professional practice as a spiritual healer and counsellor numerous times, as I always knew I could help people in that way. My first serious attempt was after a move back to Australia when I was around thirty. It was before the internet, so I placed a small advertisement in a local newspaper. It never got off the ground. One of the problems was that I looked very young for my age, and people found it difficult to believe that such a young person could help them. Indeed, I could have helped them, but my professional practice had to stew in my auric field for quite some time.

My Healing Room

As explained in my first book, *The Love of Being Loving*, one evening when I was forty-five, I suddenly became aware of a dawning idea. It was time to set up my practice as a spiritual healer and counsellor. I was ready to expand my spiritual influence. Something about the idea was so definite that it seemed impossible for it not to work. I had been working with a spiritual healer and teacher, John Hargreaves, for about two years. I didn't know that when I got the idea to start my practice, it was only a matter of weeks before his passing. It was as if the candle of healer was passed from senior to junior (perhaps unknowingly, but passed nevertheless). I also got the idea to start writing my first book about the teachings that had most influenced and helped me, including that current teacher.

Getting my practice off the ground was successful this time. It may not have been flying high financially, but it was healing and helping people, and that is the best kind of flying for a healer. I also had the opportunity to work part-time for a few years as a counsellor at a Christian Science-based school. As Christian Science is highly healing-oriented, it was a rare opportunity to combine my healing work and counselling qualifications in a school environment.

My private practice steadily progressed, and I also slowly wrote my book, partly using content written for clients and groups. The book took three years to write. It then sat in my drawer for another three years because the few publishers I approached weren't interested. Eventually, I decided to publish it independently. I pulled it out of the drawer and edited it for another two years. After an eight-year journey, it was finally published. Little did I know I had entered new terrain and would soon throw myself wholeheartedly into the author world.

HELL'S BELLS—THE MAD HEALER

After nearly ten years of my spiritual healing and counselling practice, I moved from the quieter, conservative outer suburbs to a vibrant, gentrified, inner-city suburb. The move was for personal reasons, but I thought the new environment would be perfect for my practice. It wasn't. It wasn't really the fault of the new suburb. Other things had changed along the way. I was writing more. As we have limited time and energy, I felt I could reach more people with writing than with a one-on-one private practice. I didn't deliberately choose the change. It just evolved that way. Writing was a more efficient way of sharing what was in me, what I had learned, and what I felt would help people.

Moving from one thing to another usually involves a period of choppy sailing when we can't quite tell if we are doing something wrong (that we previously did right) or if the thing itself needs changing. That's where the *mad healer* comes in. I was becoming reluctant to book clients in. When they came, I felt less than enthusiastic, which had certainly never been the case. I can't remember my last client, but I do remember my behaviour.

After the counselling half of the session, the client relaxed on the massage table for the healing half. Some creativity is expected in healing sessions as it is intuitive and the Spirit leads you. However, my imagination got a little out of hand. I had small bells that I used to gently signal the end of the session. After about ten minutes, I started chiming the bells above the client's lying body. Not too offensive. But then I got carried away. The bell ringing became louder and louder, more and more insistent and intense. I began chanting along with the urgently ringing bells, up and down the client's body, round and round the massage table. The client, fortunately, had their eyes closed. I joined the bell chiming and chanting with vigorous dancing. Not ballroom dancing. More like Sufi dancing. Arms flinging. Body twirling. My dancing self and professional self got swept up in one chiming, chanting, flailing body of energetic exuberance. Finally, the time was up, and...I stopped.

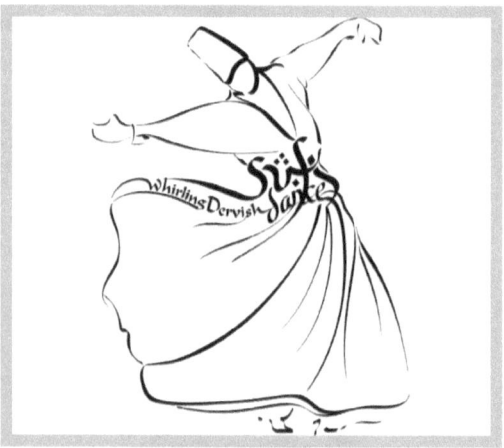

I had no idea what effect it had on the client. They never said anything, and I never asked them. But after that session, I said to myself, "Hell's bells! My days of healing are over."

When I recently looked up the meaning of *hell's bells,* the dictionary said it was an exclamation of annoyance and gave the example of this sentence: *"Hell's bells, Don, you're being unreasonable!"* My family call me Don, so I thought it was a very suitable sentence for my bell-ringing situation. It may have been fun and intensely expressive, and maybe the client even got their healing from it, but it wasn't professional or reasonable. So, after ten years, I stopped my healing and counselling practice and dedicated myself to full-time writing.

MOVING AGAIN

Close to another decade passed, and another move came. My youngest child moved out of home, so I moved out to the country, which was a long-held dream. My roots are rural, but all my adult years have been spent in city living.

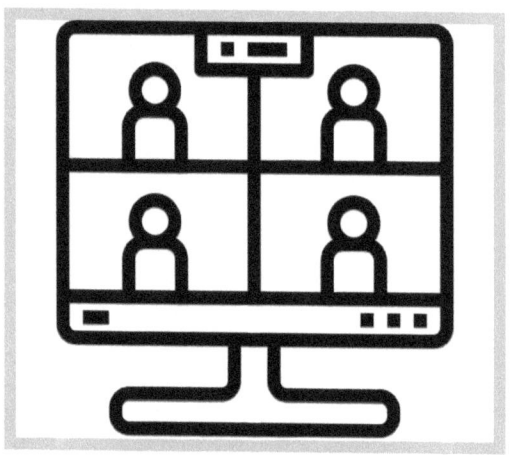

After settling into my delightful little rural hometown, I attended an online class with a master qigong teacher from New York, Robert Peng. He was new to me, and so were his classes. As if by a strike of lightning, and for no logical reason, an idea struck as soon as I finished the Zoom class. It was more than an idea. It was a *knowingness*. I knew it was time to restart my spiritual healing and counselling practice. This idea had not even vaguely entered my mind for the past ten years of full-time writing. It was not that I occasionally played with the idea. I thought my time in private practice was done. Clearly not.

My re-entry into the profession came with the new ability to provide *online* sessions and classes, which suited me perfectly in my rural location. Three things are foundational in providing a spiritual service:

1. The most important is to **care**. If the practitioner doesn't care, nothing good will happen.
2. Secondly, the spiritual counsellor must **see and understand** where the person is developmentally, their blockages, and how to best help them move forward. This empathic and largely psychic ability is often born within someone, as it was within me. However, the ability automatically increases in all spiritual seekers.
3. Thirdly, we must be sincere, dedicated, and **devoted practitioners** of the spiritual path ourselves. Without a strong presence of the Divine in us, we cannot help other people to ignite that presence within them. The Divine in the practitioner is the very thing that helps people to heal, grow, and gain their happiness.

PERFECTLY PATIENT WITH PEOPLE

We must be patient with people who come our way for help. People are often delusional, repetitive, depressing, fanciful, reactive, arrogant, lazy, ungrateful, idiotic, and/or obnoxious. The ego is, by nature, all these qualities. However, those who have decided to enter the healing path deserve help and patience. Most will not be "perfect" students—intelligent, receptive, humble, grateful, self-correcting, and inspired. And if they are, they probably won't be with you for long because they will have a grand purpose.

HEALERS DO NOT HEAL

Our intention is to ignite spiritual energy in those who come to us by our presence. It is the yogic way of initiation or transfer of vibration. The presence of a more advanced spiritual individual automatically ignites some things in others. It is the most effective approach to relieving suffering and long-term growth.

Healers do not heal. They radiate a particular type of vibration, which another person can then accept or reject. In this sense, the healer is simply being themselves, which is neither tiring nor depleting. It is not up to us what other people do with the energy field we give off. If they feel happier and better in our presence and like that feeling, they may choose to mirror the energy field, which automatically brings healing. They may choose not to because they're too busy with their problems to see or feel it, or they may still like their suffering.

CHAPTER 21

primary practices

The spiritual path involves two primary practices.

1. The first is **dissolving our problems.** That requires a lot of going into our emotions, memories, and pain. It is called by different names—burning karma, riding out emotions, going into oneself, dissolving memories. It is not a comfortable process because it means allowing angry, sad, and fearful thoughts to come up and be clearly seen so they can dissolve.
2. The second is **dissolving our ego.** That involves merging with our spiritual identity. Again, it can be uncomfortable. It is highly comfortable to our soul, but our ego can (and probably will) experience it as life-threatening. But not to worry because the discomfort is only temporary, and the blessed result is permanent.

These practices are incredibly fruitful. Our problems will dramatically decrease, and our well-being will splendidly increase. However, both practices require courage and humility. It is best to have the guidance and protection of a teacher, but the process itself will guide you.

MYSTIC

I am a mystic.
Come, come.
We will mystic together.

The mystic matters.
The mysterious matters.
The mysterious knows me.
I know it.

We are friends.
Sometimes enemies.
But not mysterious.
Known.

I am a mystic.
I am.

CHAPTER 22

choose consciousness

The pivotal thing we must do in our life journey is to become conscious or awake. For most people who succeed, it's a gradual process, but it can have abrupt stages. The beginning of a big shift can be quite painful and disorienting. We suddenly realise how little we know but don't have the Divine-knowingness to replace it yet.

I made my biggest consciousness shift at age twenty-two. I realised I didn't know what I was thinking most of the time, and for that matter, neither did anyone else. However, other people were neither aware of this nor did they want to be. Having become distinctly aware of my lack of consciousness, I went through a stage of constantly looking at my thoughts. This stage can take some years before it becomes second nature. The process affected me in two observable and obvious ways:

1. It made me **quiet** in terms of interaction with other people. Once you see the stupidity and floating randomness of most human interaction, you are not so keen to participate in its roundabout, merry-go-round nature. I went from being a bubbly, chatty young person to a more introverted, silentish adult. I remember an ex-boyfriend telling me at a social gathering, "Well, you certainly have the 'Be still and know that I am God' thing going on." He belonged to the same spiritual community I had belonged to, thus the Bible reference. He wasn't criticising my new personality, although it would have been entirely understandable if he had concerns about my sudden silence. He was referencing it in terms of spiritual progress, which was entirely correct, although probably unfathomable to him at that point.
2. The second observable way it affected me was that I went through a stage of **speaking slowly**. I didn't intend that to happen, but when we are

> watching our thoughts and words, in the beginning, the words can take a while to come out in the proper order and with the right meaning. An au pair said rather bluntly, "You always speak so slowly and carefully. Can you talk quicker?" After that, I tried to speed up the pace of my words a little, although I think it was only time that modified it back to a regular speech pattern.

See yourself as being entirely awake and aware. Be mindful that most of humanity is neither awake nor aware. Most people do not understand that this is even a possibility. Our greatest gift as humans is to be conscious and live life with awareness. We have a choice. What a blessing it is to choose consciousness.

NOTHING MUCH

Those intent on the spiritual path will find that they have periods during their life when stretches of solitude are both desired and necessary. If the push is strong enough, then one way or another, the solitary stretches will be organised.

It can become a little peculiar to explain what one does with one's time when much of it is spent on the inner world. It can appear as if we are doing nothing because, sometimes, nothing much is happening outwardly. While the concept of *doing* will have been transformed for the spiritual person, others are generally *doing*-oriented and want to know what you have been doing, too. My usual answer over the years has been, "Oh, just the normal things." That tends to work. The person will look slightly puzzled and feel as if they ought to know what "normal things" are, and then they generally continue with their conversation. After all, most people are not that interested in what *you* are doing. They are interested in what *they* are doing.

We are not trying to be special, something more, or better than anyone else in our inner solitariness. We are simply being. We are returning to our original nature of happiness and peace. Enlightenment doesn't mean being more and more, but less and less. The body is still there. The mind is still there. The personality is still there. The life experiences are still there. Most of the relationships are still there. But the soul is transformed into something that becomes immensely fluid and connected with the ultimate life force. It is an irresistible pull. If it comes your way, you have no choice. You'll have to follow. It's just a matter of timing. You cannot rush it. Nor would you want to because you will find yourself out of your depth. Do what you are capable of now, and that will transform and bless you beyond conventional belief.

CHAPTER 23
translating

I went to my local Chinese massage shop. They have a rotating stream of masseurs who come from China on a three-month visa. The young masseur said in broken English, "Your arm is bubbly."

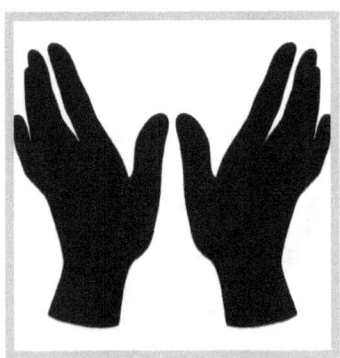

"Yes," I said, "it's too much work on the computer."

In such situations, I often make myself sound like a clerical worker because I don't want to discuss being a writer.

After a few minutes, he said, "You are a writer."

The chances of being a writer out of the thousands of jobs one could do on a computer must be minimal.

I laughed and said, "How did you know? You must be psychic."

He answered, "I could tell from your..."

He hesitated as he searched for the right word on his phone translator.

"Temperament," he said.

Before this conversation, I hadn't said a word to him, which made me more sure of his extrasensory abilities. Although, sitting there silently and introspectively would probably indicate an inward-looking nature, and writers are generally introspective.

"One day, I would like to be a writer," he said.

I wanted to explain that he should write from the place in him that "knew" things about people, but the idea was too subtle for a translator to explain. Regardless, there is a good chance that the psychic part of him picked up on my intention, and it will help him on his way.

CHAPTER 24

fear is your friend

Fear is your friend, not your enemy. When fear and anxiety arise, they are trying to tell you that something in your belief system and how you approach life is not in your best interest. Something is not in accord with who you are and what you deep-down want for your life. Make the deep-down visible, and you will be a happier being.

When you feel anxious, don't then create more fear by feeling anxious about being anxious. Tell yourself that if you feel anxious, your consciousness is trying to tell you that you need to be more in line with your true nature. The anxiety is simply a sign to let you know that something is misaligned. Use your anxiety as a tool to help you find your path in life and set up your inner structure. You want your interior self to give you balance, productivity, and fulfilment. Anxiety is a message to you, not a frightening, unsolvable problem.

Search for the underlying basis of the anxiety, and you'll find what is out of balance. The fundamental structure of your being is asking you to correct it for your benefit. Remember that change for the better is what you want to do. The anxiety becomes a tool that you curiously and enthusiastically use to your advantage. It's exciting when we know we are going to learn something important and improve our lives. Anxiety can be a tool that is working to get you exactly where you want to go.

CHAPTER 25

awake and aware

The most fundamental thing we need to do as evolving beings is to wake up. At a certain point in our evolution, we realise that the vast majority of people are not awake or conscious. They don't know what they're doing, thinking, or saying. All sorts of things happen to them for seemingly no apparent reason. They get sick, have accidents, worry all the time, and their fear is enormous.

At some point in their evolution, everyone starts to wake up and look at themselves without filters. It won't be this lifetime for many (if not most), but that is the nature of evolution. For those who are seekers, it will be this lifetime. Once we become conscious, we learn how to create the life we want and radiate the energy we desire. We learn how to create things in a way that's in harmony with life, and then all of life works with us. We will understand which elements to bring into our creations and relationships so that they flourish, blossom, and benefit ourselves and others. We become masters of our destiny.

Not only is most of humanity not awake nor aware, but they do not even realise it is possible. However, our greatest gift as humans is that we can be conscious and live life with awareness. We have a choice, and what a blessing that is to our life. Consciousness is the path to alleviating every problem. When issues come our way, we will know how to receive the right ideas for dealing with those problems most effectively. Suffering will be hugely reduced until it is, one day, eliminated. Practise seeing yourself as being awake in all the various situations of your life. Practice is the path to eventual mastery.

CHAPTER 26

humans are aliens too

People have long pondered whether life exists elsewhere in the universe and whether aliens are real. Given the incomprehensible size, nature, and complexity of existence, it would be arrogant and unintelligent to assume that we are the only place with life and the only beings capable of thought, action, and consciousness. To believe that other forms of life are nonexistent is like thinking there is nowhere else if one lived in early Europe. It is simply limited vision and experience.

It is also arrogant to conceptualise that we are the *proper* mould of creation and that everyone and everything else is an aberration or alien. No, in the grand scheme of creation, humans are aliens, too. Or perhaps one could say there are no aliens—only vast, infinitely intricate creatures of creation.

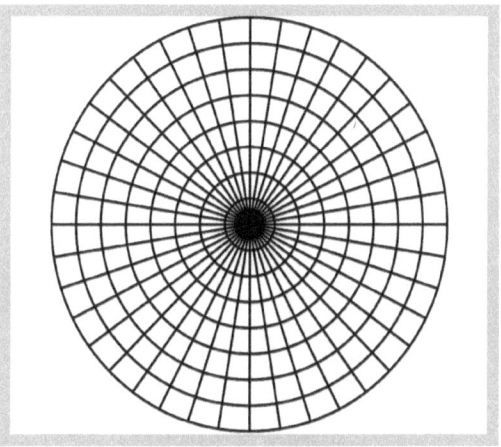

It is likely that somewhere (perhaps numerous places), there are planets very similar to Earth, with a similar sun support system, making an ideal home for creatures like us. It is also likely that many places, planes, and beings, which we can neither see, understand or imagine, exist as alternate realities. We can't yet travel to other worlds, and it seems that they can't travel here, but maybe they can. For creatures who are evolved enough, travel is not only physical but also mental and energetic.

CHAPTER 27

spiritual teachers

LONG AGO AWAKENINGS

When visiting my mother in a small country town many years ago, I casually looked at her little, decades-old book collection. I came across several yellowed, dusty books by a Catholic priest. A memory rushed forward. One of them had been the catalyst for my first significant spiritual and psychological self-awareness.

In 1972, when I was twelve, my father attended a staff development day for suburban bank managers. It was based on the then-new field of psychology. My father was not interested in self-development or spirituality. However, a forward-thinking CEO must have recognised the benefit of exposing his managers to psychology.

Coming home with the freshly published book by the priest-author, my father told me all about the staff development day and the field of psychology. I took to it like a long-lost friend. If he was enthused, I was more so. I confiscated the book to my room, not to part with it for many years. Thus, at the formative age of twelve, I began my journey into the impact of thought on life experience.

ONE LITTLE YES

A spiritual teacher is no little thing. They can help us move forward enormously and save us many lifetimes of work and the equivalent amount of suffering. Teachers are proven not by their words or even their actions. They are teachers because they have the necessary energetic power to transform lives.

Recognising and honouring the people who help us is important and karmically correct. True teachers do not need recognition, but taking something from someone without acknowledging where it came from creates bad karma. Worse is hating someone and then trying to use them. I can recall people who have made themselves my enemy, taken my ideas, and tried to use them for their own benefit. Of course, it doesn't work because the person they are and the ideas they are sprouting do not match. It's particularly immature to hate someone and simultaneously try to benefit from them. What could they possibly expect but bad karma?

The whole point of a spiritual teacher is that they make us grow, which in turn leads to improved happiness. Sometimes, we will feel distinctly uncomfortable as that is the soil for growth. But the discomfort is only temporary. If the student is not growing, the teacher is not doing their job, or the student is not doing theirs. If it is the former, find another teacher. Countless, willing, and able teachers and teachings swirl around us, trying to tempt us with their kind, intelligent tenderness.

A spiritual teacher is a presence and way-shower. They do not fix or change anyone. Their energy, heightened from many lifetimes of practice and dedication, becomes a pulsing light to which others are drawn. The light of those drawn to them increases, and they, in turn, become a light to those around them. It is nonpersonal and automatic. All it needs is a *yes* from any sufferer seeking a way out. One little *yes* leads to disproportionate growth and life improvement.

SHINING HEART

May all the enlightened beings
who have ever walked
the face of this planet
shine their love into your heart

so that our world becomes
a place where
no child is hungry,
no one fears the invasion of their home,

Mother Nature doesn't have to
forgive our foolish selfishness,
and everyone has
absolute freedom

to be their most
individual,
enthusiastic,
and evolved self.

CHAPTER 28

garden your consciousness

Imagine that you have been given a garden to work with. It's not an empty patch of land. It's an old, overgrown garden. Many beautiful plants are struggling and hidden under the overgrowth. You have time, so you decide to throw yourself into it. You could employ someone else to do it, but what fun would that be? Anyway, they probably wouldn't make it the way you want. You might not know yourself how you want it until you are immersed in the project.

Every day, when you wake up, you are excited to work on your project and see its progress. It's a large garden and hard work, but you're committed to it. It's particularly tough in the beginning because you are not used to the physical work and are quite unfit. The soil hasn't been watered for a long time, and initially, it's like watering concrete. With gentle watering, it softens, and you can start working with it. You begin weeding. Every time you start a new section, you have to work out which are weeds and which are plants because you don't know what is planted there, and your gardening knowledge is elementary. You make many mistakes and sometimes kill what you later discover to be good plants. But you tell yourself not to focus on what has died but on what is still alive.

It takes six months for it to look like a garden, not a rubbish tip. It takes a year for the seasons to work their magic on the resuscitated flora. It takes five years to turn it into a special place of beauty, but you have patience. Being patient was not difficult because every step was so rewarding and bore such good fruit.

Take up this gardening project with your mind. Once you have dedicated yourself to clearing, cleaning, weeding, and watering it, working out what belongs and what doesn't, and discovering how to cooperate with the forces around you, you will be well on your way to turning the garden of yourself into a beauty. You will have entered a new, exhilarating time in your evolution and will end up with a stunning consciousness garden that benefits many others as well as yourself.

closing prayer

Dedicate yourself to being awake and aware.
Fill your heart with love.
Have love for everyone you come across.
And feel that everyone has love for you.

If they don't have love for you,
it's their problem.
At least, for you, there is only love.
Don't let the shadow of lovelessness fall on
   your mind.

Feel that you're going out into the world
with little lights inside you—
the things you love, that you can do,
and that you're interested in.

Those little lights will grow more and
bring happiness to you, your loved ones,
all those you come upon,
and even think of.

Sweet Spirit Series

The **Sweet Spirit Series** is a heartfelt offering for those seeking healing, clarity, and inner peace. Through **gentle wisdom and soulful insight**, these books invite us to honour our body, transform our relationships, and live from the quiet strength of spirit.

In *Touched by Love*, we explore the deep interconnection between our **physical well-being, emotional life, and spiritual awakening**. We are reminded that love is not only a feeling but a healing power—one that brings balance to every part of our being.

In *Love Matters*, we continue the journey through three sacred gateways:

- *Physical Matters* — respecting the body as a temple of **truth**
- *People Matters* — allowing relationships to become vessels of **growth**
- *Mystic Matters* — opening to the silent beauty of the **soul**

SWEET SPIRIT SERIES

These books are a companion for those who long to live with **grace, simplicity, and spiritual depth.** They remind us that everything in life is part of the path—and that love, when truly understood, transforms everything it touches.

about the author

Donna Goddard is a spiritual author whose work blends clarity, devotion, and metaphysical insight. With more than twenty published books across spiritual nonfiction, fiction, poetry, and children's literature, she writes to uplift consciousness and offer healing through words.

Donna's Facebook author page has over 400,000 followers from around the world, and her YouTube channel has received more than three million views. Her books are read by spiritual seekers globally and are known for their honesty, poetic style, and transformative energy.

Her writing is an offering—to help others awaken their own inner spirit, trust its guidance, and create a life of depth, beauty, and quiet joy.

All links at https://linktr.ee/donnagoddard

RATINGS AND REVIEWS

Donna would be most grateful for any ratings or reviews.

also by donna goddard

Fiction
Waldmeer Series: A Spiritual Fiction Series
Nanima Series: Spiritual Fiction
Riverland Series (children's fiction 6 to 9 years)
The Fox Tales (children's fiction 8 to 12 years)

Nonfiction
Love and Devotion Series
Sweet Spirit Series
Dance: A Spiritual Affair
Writing: A Spiritual Voice
Strange Words: Poems and Prayers
Love's Longing
Master of Me: Meditations

www.ingramcontent.com/pod-product-compliance
Lightning Source LLC
Chambersburg PA
CBHW031230290426
44109CB00012B/239